something to wag about

Judy McWhorter artfully weaves spiritual principles and truths of God's word into inspirational and tender moments in *Devotions for Dog Lovers,* a collection of insightful and humorous modern-day parables that will touch both dog lovers and their friends. It's more than a good story book, it's a window into our souls.

—Thomas Jones, Minister of Education,
Roswell Street Baptist Church, Marietta, Georgia

Judy McWhorter not only loves dogs, she loves God! Her devotion to her dogs is matched by her devotion to God, and both are seen in the pages of this book. If you are a God-lover and dog-lover, you will be inspired by these devotions.

—Dr. Randy White, Pastor,
First Baptist Church of Katy, TX

I imitated Jesus' method of using parables for my daily radio programs. Judy uses her dogs to articulate God's truths. Dogs hold no resentments, are not jealous, are always playful, and always know and love their master. They communicate the beauty of their Maker.

—Dr. Paul Finkenbinder, Veteran Missionary,
Assemblies of God

DEVOTIONS *for* Dog Lovers

Judy McWhorter

Devotions for Dog Lovers

life lessons from canine companions

Tate Publishing & *Enterprises*

Published by Tate Publishing & Enterprises, LLC
127 E. Trade Center Terrace | Mustang, Oklahoma 73064 USA
1.888.361.9473 | www.tatepublishing.com

Tate Publishing is committed to excellence in the publishing industry. The company reflects the philosophy established by the founders, based on Psalm 68:11,
"The Lord gave the word and great was the company of those who published it."

Cover design by Amber Gulilat
Interior design by Stephanie Woloszyn

Published in the United States of America

ISBN: 978-1-61566-265-4
1. Religion / Christian Life / Devotional
2. Religion / Christian Life / Inspirational
09.11.12

to my dear mother,

Louise,

who didn't mind being "Granny"
to my furry, four-footed children.

Mother

Acknowledgments

I am forever indebted to my family and friends who contributed to this book through the tales of their own canine companions. They have provided me feedback in reading my drafts and have patiently sat and listened as I read the devotionals to them. They have encouraged me through their responses to the truths I have tried to convey as I myself have experienced them. The names are many but must be recognized. Thanks to Marianna Lott, who has been my friend since childhood, as close as a sister, for her steady belief that I could bring this book to fruition, and who lives with BeBe. Thanks to Vicki Broach, who has been my Chief Encourager, and who lives with Scooter. Thanks to Dana Wessels, for her patience and encouragement, and who lived with Freckles. Thanks to Cate Campbell, who gave me objective feedback, and who lives with Cupcake. Thanks to Mary Nan Johnson, my cousin and the closest relative I have to a sister, for her spiritual insight and prayers, and whose daughter, Lauren, lives with Molly. Thanks to Carol Lemm, for her inspiration and love, and who lives with Wylie and Shelby. Thanks to Lorie Cutbirth, with whom I shared my first thoughts of writing this book, and who lives with Marcie. Thanks to Scott Ludwick, whose excitement for this project gave me cheer and encouragement, and who lived with Tick. Thanks to my niece Regina McWhorter, whose faith warms my heart, and who lived with Tasha. Thanks to my nephew Brandon McWhorter, who amuses me with his playful love for Getty, and for whom I harbor great love as my brother's firstborn son. Thanks to Brandon's brothers, my nephews, Kevin McWhorter and Vincent McWhorter, and their wives, Sandi and Regina, as well as Brandon's late wife, Reagan, who continually offered up encouragement to me and who understood when I needed to spend time on this book rather than visiting with their families.

I will be forever grateful that Trinity Tate at Tate Publishing Company read my devotionals and caught my desire to offer these up as edification and encouragement to the saints and as a means to draw to Christ those who have yet to believe. I have appreciated the assistance of all the staff at Tate Publishing for their excitement for this project and as they have guided me through this first book adventure.

May those who have shared in this journey be blessed as much as I have for having taken it.

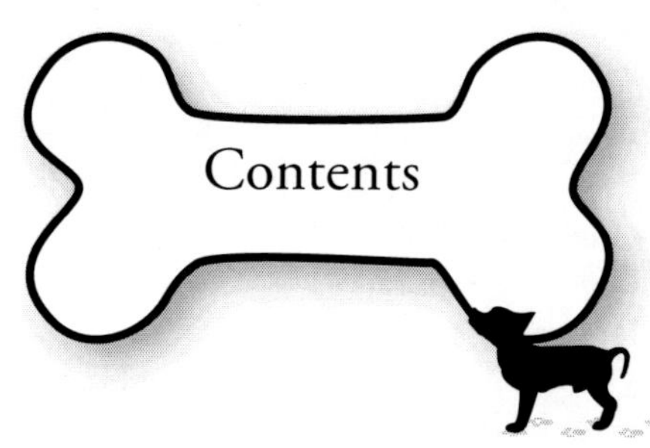

Contents

Introduction

When I was six, my father left our family, so I grew up for the most part without an earthly example of the Heavenly Father. My mother, however, was a deeply devout Christian, and she provided a wonderful Christian home for my brother and me. My earliest memories are of going into the kitchen after Mother left for work and seeing her Bible propped up at an angle on the table, so she could read it as she ate breakfast. How blessed I am for that image in my memory!

Somewhere along the way, my maternal instincts gene for babies and children failed to kick in "timely." Instead, this canine affinity gene bloomed, and I have found great contentment and fulfillment in being the Leader of the Pack of my canine "children." Just like human children do for my friends, my canine children have brought me joy and heartache. They know how to tell me when they are hungry, thirsty, or need affection. When I am on the phone for an extended period of time, they begin to act up, just as kids do to regain their parent's attention when the parent has been on the phone too long (in the kids' opinion, of course).

As demonstrated so many times in the Bible, God speaks to us right where we are—right in the middle of our everyday life. Moses was out tending sheep when God spoke to him through the burning bush. Peter and Andrew were fishing out on the Sea of Galilee when Jesus called them to be his disciples. Saul (later Paul) was on the way to Damascus to arrest some of the new believers when Jesus stopped him dead in his tracks to speak to him. I guess it should have come as no surprise to me, then, that God would teach me lessons through my everyday life of living with and caring for my canine companions.

Paul spoke of Jesus as our Master when he said this to the Ephesians: "And masters, treat your slaves in the same way. Do not threaten them, since you know that he who is both their Master and yours is in heaven, and there is no favoritism with him" (Ephesians 6:9). Jesus himself used the comparison of the heavenly Master with an earthly master in many of his parables. As Leader of the Pack, I am my dogs' master, even so as Jesus is my heavenly Master. It is my prayer that you will find relevant truths for your life as I have recorded my experiences with my canine companions in this book. May the truths expressed draw you to a closer relationship with our heavenly Master, so that he may say to us at heaven's door, "Well done, thou good and faithful servant" (Matthew 25:21).

Always Keep Your Eyes on the Master

> And Peter answered him and said, "Lord, if it be thou, bid me come unto thee on the water." And he said, "Come." And when Peter was come down out of the ship, he walked on the water, to go to Jesus. But when he saw the wind boisterous, he was afraid; and beginning to sink, he cried, saying, "Lord, save me." And immediately Jesus stretched forth his hand, and caught him, and said unto him, "O thou of little faith, wherefore didst thou doubt?"
>
> Matthew 14:28–31

One of the first things I ever noticed about my dogs is how they *watch* me—all the time. I may be reading, watching television, or working at the computer, but if I happen to look up, I will find a pair of eyes fixed on me. They aren't signaling a need to go outside or to be fed; they are simply watching me, alert to my slightest move and ready to respond in an instant. I am the focal point of their world, and nothing is more important to them than me. It's so very sweet and pure. Their gaze moves me to pet them or to give them some kind of attention, and I am pleased to do it.

Of course, the message here is that *our* eyes should be fixed on the Master. They will be if he is the center of our world, just as I am the center of each of my dogs' worlds. In our scripture, Peter was excited to see Jesus! Peter could think of nothing more than to get close to Jesus, and at the Master's invitation and without hesitation or regard for the storm, he got out of the boat and began to walk on the water toward Jesus. Peter walked on water! He obviously must have started looking around him, aware of the phenomenon, because the scripture tells us that he then "saw the wind boisterous." At the moment that Jesus was no longer his focus—that his eyes were no longer fixed on Jesus—Peter's faith failed and fear set in.

Note that it was not until he became *afraid* that he began to sink in the water. When you're sinking, survival instinct kicks in, and all you can do is cry out to be saved. Peter was not moved to have a discussion with Jesus about the elements of the storm and their effect on his balance on the water. He did not try to reason with Jesus for another chance, nor did he point out that only he out of all the disciples had had enough faith to get out of the boat in the first place. Peter recognized his peril and cried out for Jesus to save him, and Jesus responded *immediately.* What a lesson to learn!

Yes, we *should* keep our eyes fixed on Jesus (see Hebrews 12:2), but we are human and fallible. Once we become aware that Jesus is no longer our focus and that life has become intolerable because of it, there is nothing to do but cry out to Jesus! And we are promised that he will respond *immediately.* Hallelujah! What a loving Savior!

Heavenly Father,

I want to keep an unswerving gaze upon you. Let me look neither to the right nor to the left but focus completely on you.

Left to Our Own, We Will Stray

> All we like sheep have gone astray; we have turned every one to his own way; and the Lord hath laid on him the iniquity of us all.
>
> Isaiah 53:6

Every dog owner's nightmare—an open gate. Whether it was left open by the cable guy, the meter reader, or even one of the family, a gate ajar beckons the most content backyard dog to explore the outside world. The temptation to discover new sights and smells is overwhelming, and out they dash into newfound freedom.

We know they love us. We know they love being with us. And yet the average dog will just go running off without hesitation. How many sad stories can we tell about our precious pets who never found their way back home once they escaped the safety of the backyard? How many more sad tales do we know about those sweet pups who met with mortal disaster after escaping? We wish we could protect them 24/7 from placing themselves in danger. If we could only help them understand that the "grass isn't greener" on the other side of the fence!

I know God must feel the same way about us. Left to *our* own, we humans *will* stray. We naturally find the path of danger and undoing through so many of Satan's enticements. We know we are much better off within the safety and contentment of God's will, yet we knowingly flirt with ungodly thoughts and actions. We are certain we can find the way back to God after a "quick detour" that appears deceptively interesting. Yet sometimes all it takes is a quick detour to set us on a course of ruin from which recovery is nothing less than a miracle.

Couched in the middle of one of the prophecies concerning Jesus and his redemptive death is today's focal verse. It's as if Isaiah needed to stress *why* Jesus must come and die for our sins. His comparison of us to sheep bids note. In Isaiah's day of shepherds and their flocks of sheep, it was well known that sheep had little sense of direction, and if they wandered off from the flock, there was no hope that they would find their way back on their own. So are we, cut off from our Shepherd, unable to find our way back on our own.

The shepherd would leave his flock to go find a stray sheep. Omnipresent God does not have to leave the rest of his flock to find us. He reaches to us with outstretched arms, beckoning us to his life and his love. He surely must want to speak in a loud voice to us and say, "Come back! The grass isn't greener. There is shelter and peace within my will."

Dear God,

Call to my mind the remembrance of my excursions outside your "backyard." May I not stray from your will as my dogs stray from their yard, but rather cling to you and the safety and contentment of your will.

We Can Get Dirty on Our Own, but It Takes the Master to Clean Us Up

For whom the Lord loveth he chasteneth.

Hebrews 12:6

Getting dirty is natural, and dogs don't seem to need help getting dirty. In fact, a good roll in a pile of dirt is usually very enjoyable to them! I think their tolerance for dirt must be very high, because a quick body shake of the fur seems to cast off enough surface dirt to satisfy them. But we humans have much higher standards for cleanliness, and if our furry friends are going to share our home, they need to be clean to *our* standards, not theirs! Hence, we brush them, we bathe them, and we spend our hard-earned dollars on professional grooming. We do this not only because we recognize the value of cleanliness but also because we love them as a part of the family.

In Hebrews 12, the chapter of our focal verse, we are encouraged to "lay aside … the sin which doth so easily beset us." Yes! Sin *does* so easily find me! Or, rather, I suppose, I so easily find sin. Just like my dogs, I don't seem to need help dirtying myself spiritually. A little indulgement of resentment here, a small dose of envy there, a few days missed in the Word, and *bam,* there you have it—a very dirty soul that needs God's cleansing and forgiveness.

Sometimes God's cleansing involves disciplining us. He does this because he loves us *as his own children.* We are reminded in Hebrews 12 that any father who loves his children disciplines them. We know that disciplining our children is necessary so that they can function as a cooperating member of society. The other day I had lunch with some of my family and their four-year-old didn't like the food that was being served. To demonstrate her distress, she opened her mouth and allowed the food to fall out of it directly onto the table! Naturally, this necessitated a trip to her room where table manners were quietly but firmly discussed. If her father didn't love her, he wouldn't be concerned with her behavior.

Hebrews 12 tells us that if God didn't chasten us, we would not be his true sons and daughters and that his discipline is for our good so that we might share in his holiness. Just as we want our dogs to be clean to share our home, God wants us to be clean to share in his own holiness!

Dear Father,

Thank you that you love me enough to chasten me. In my heart I truly want your discipline so that I can be counted as your own child and share in your holiness.

Getting Cleaned Up Usually Isn't Fun, but We Feel So Much Better Afterward

> Purge me with hyssop, and I shall be clean: wash me, and I shall be whiter than snow.
>
> Psalm 51:7

I've never had a dog that enjoyed getting a bath. A clean dog is absolutely necessary for health reasons, but the looks that have come from my canine friends as they stand there dripping wet, totally humiliated, could argue that they are best left to their own comfortable dirt! The other day I declared war on all "varmints" inhabiting my three dogs' fur. The war required a vigilant combing and administering antivarmint pills and topicals. By the time it was all over, none of my usually loving dogs would even come near me! The upside of that difficult afternoon was a restful, quiet night free of pacing and scratching.

In today's verse, David's contrition over his adultery with Bathsheba caused him to cry out to God to cleanse him from his sin. David asked to be cleansed with the herb hyssop. Hyssop has a slightly bitter taste and is so strong that it has been used as a poultice to reduce the risk of tetanus infection. It can be taken internally for use as either a laxative or an expectorant. Neither of these uses, laxative or expectorant, calls to mind pleasant experiences. However, sometimes this is necessary to cleanse the body, much in the same manner that God can cleanse a repentant soul. True repentance can be very painful. However, once purged—forgiven—the repentant David likened himself to fresh, white snow. And who isn't delighted and captivated by the sight of pure-white snow? So, the next time you need a spiritual bath, call out to God in repentance, as David did. God will cleanse your soul, and you will be spiritually refreshed, just like the beauty of fresh, white snow.

Dear God,

I acknowledge and confess my sins to you. Forgive me and let me know the beauty of your cleansing forgiveness.

Our Gifts to Our Doggies Can Never Compare to the Master's Gifts to Us

> If ye then, being evil, know how to give good gifts unto your children, how much more shall your Father which is in heaven give good things to them that ask him?
>
> Matthew 7:11

One of the earliest spiritual truths that manifested itself to me as a dog owner was a new understanding of today's verse. I had always understood it mentally. But, oh, how my heart flooded with joy the first time I gave a chew-bone to Chuckie, my first Siberian Husky. He was totally delighted with it and wagged his tail in profuse appreciation for my generosity and thoughtfulness. It was just a chew-bone—the first of many! But he loved it and each one that came after it.

That has been a common trait of all my precious dogs. They are so *thankful* and take such pleasure in any kind of little treat. And, except for being careful not to spoil them too much, I try to give them "good gifts" as often as I can. I love how their eyes light up in expectation and how they bark in anticipation of receiving a treat. I'm sure that parents have this same reaction when hearing the delighted shriek of a child at the sight of a toy she has longed for.

So if we can be good to our children, or to our doggies, *how much more* will the heavenly Father be good to us? I believe that God actually *enjoys* blessing us. The Bible is replete with promises that God has made to us so that we may have an abundant life. All we have to do is open ourselves to him. Here are just a few of his promises to consider.

His Presence

Jeremiah 29:11–13: "For I know the thoughts that I think toward you, saith the Lord, thoughts of peace, and not of evil, to give you an expected end. Then shall ye call upon me, and ye shall go and pray unto me, and I will hearken unto you. And ye shall seek me, and find me, when ye shall search for me with all your heart."

Forgiveness and Healing

2 Chronicles 7:14: "If my people, which are called by my name, shall humble themselves, and pray, and seek my face, and turn from their wicked ways; then will I hear from heaven, and will forgive their sin, and will heal their land."

His Return

2 Thessalonians 4:16–17: "For the Lord himself shall descend from heaven with a shout, with the voice of the archangel, and with the trump of God: and the dead in Christ shall rise

first: Then we which are alive and remain shall be caught up together with them in the clouds, to meet the Lord in the air: and so shall we ever be with the Lord."

Eternal Joy

Revelation 7:17: "For the Lamb which is in the midst of the throne shall feed them, and shall lead them unto living fountains of waters: and God shall wipe away all tears from their eyes."

Dear God,

Thank you for all you have done for me and for the blessings you so graciously bestow upon me. I know that I am not worthy and could never be worthy; I am humbled by your inexplicable love for me!

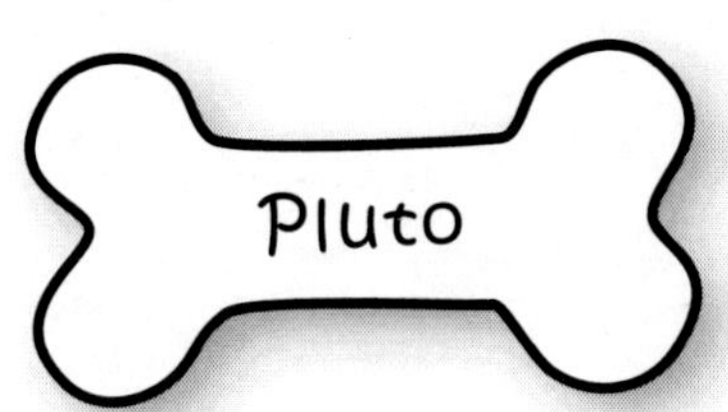
Pluto

If I Can Just Touch the Hem of the Master's Garment, I Know I'll Be Healed

> And, behold, a woman, which was diseased with an issue of blood twelve years, came behind him, and touched the hem of his garment: For she said within herself, "If I may but touch his garment, I shall be whole."
>
> Matthew 9:20–21

Pluto is probably the most loving dog I've ever had. I rescued him from my next-door neighbor when the neighbor was going to take him to the pound because he was "growing up to be such a big dog." For the first six months of his puppy life, I talked to his litter mate and him through the chain link fence. I had lost Lady, my beautiful Collie-Shepherd mix, just three weeks before I got Pluto, and the timing was right to bring in another dog.

So Pluto went from being an ignored, outdoor dog to a dog who got lots of attention and got to sleep indoors with "the family." I guess it's out of some innate gratefulness that this dog simply adores me. He positions himself where he is always touching me when we're relaxing at home. If we are sitting on opposite ends of the sofa, he scooches himself little by little till finally his head is under my arm. If he's on the floor, he'll lay his head on the bend of my foot.

I think about the lady in the Scripture passage who had the blood issue. Her only thought that day in the crowd was just to get close enough to touch the hem of Jesus' garment. She knew that she would be healed just by being close to Jesus. In like manner, our souls are healed of the influence of the world through drawing close to Jesus. The Psalmist said, "But it is good for me to draw near to God: I have put my trust in the Lord GOD, that I may declare all thy works" (Psalm 73:28). How do we draw near to God? Jesus himself gives us the example. Whenever the Son needed to commune with the Father, what did he do? He would draw himself away privately in prayer. So likewise can we draw close to God by taking time to commune with him in prayer and supplication.

Dear God,

Let me always find the time to spend with you in prayer, for I know that it is only in drawing close to you that my soul is continually healed from the onslaughts of the world.

The Master Knows Our Name

> And the Lord said unto Moses, "I will do this thing also that thou hast spoken: for thou hast found grace in my sight, and I know thee by name."
>
> Exodus 33:17

Naming a pet is often a family affair and brings with it much thought and consideration. As each precious dog has entered my life, naming him or her has followed a real process. A number of my dogs have been named after "movie star dogs," e.g., Benji, Lady, Pluto. Perhaps Pippin's name has raised the most questions from others. I named him after the obscure 1970s musical *Pippin.* The basic truth of this little-known musical is born out through the search of the protagonist for an extraordinary life, only to find it in a simple life filled with love.

Pippin is a real "Heinz 57" dog. We know there is some German Shepherd Dog and some Cocker Spaniel, and surely there must be some Beagle in him. I didn't think he was particularly handsome, just an ordinary-looking dog. But I looked at him and said, "Even though you're kind of ordinary, I think we shall have an extraordinary life together." And we have had a wonderful life together, filled with love, just like Pippin in the musical.

While we set great store by the meaning of our dogs' names, it is even more awesome to think that God knows *our* names! Note in our focal scripture that God assured Moses, "I know thee by name." Earlier in Exodus 33, God and Moses are speaking together in the tabernacle. The Scripture says that "the LORD spake unto Moses face-to-face, as a man speaketh unto his friend" (v. 11). Moses is asking God for guidance in leading Israel and for God to "consider that this nation is thy people" (v. 13). And so God replies that he would do what Moses has asked and assures Moses that he has found grace in his sight and he knows Moses by name. Jesus assures us that the very hairs of our head are numbered (Luke 12:7). That's how intimately God knows us. That's amazing! We can have joy and confidence as we come before him through the grace of Jesus that we are loved beyond comprehension and that he knows each of us by name!

Dear God,

Thank you for your all-knowing love for me. I am humbled that you know *me—you know my name, and you even know the number of hairs on my head! I can rest in the peace of knowing that I am known by the Master.*

Singing Together Celebrates Our Sameness

> Let the word of Christ dwell in you richly in all wisdom; teaching and admonishing one another in psalms and hymns and spiritual songs, singing with grace in your hearts to the Lord.
>
> Colossians 3:16

Having three dogs has produced a phenomenon that never existed with just two dogs in the house. That is the marvel of "choir practice." Sasha leads off in her soprano Siberian Husky "woo"; Pippin joins in an incessant tenor bark; and Pluto, a little unsure of where he fits in, takes an unassuming alto howl. Any passerby would certainly think something dreadful is happening to hear this raucous sound!

It normally lasts a minute or two, and then all is back to normal. This canine choir practice never ceases to make me laugh. They each bring their own particular sound to it. It's common to hear neighborhood dogs all howl together at the sound of a siren. I have heard this happens because the pitch of the siren hurts their ears. Nonetheless, howling is a dog thing. No matter how I might try to join in on "choir practice," my human howl just doesn't sound as authentic as my furry friends' howls! Some things are just unique to the species!

As Christians, we are unique. Paul urged the Colossians to celebrate together their uniqueness. He knew the value of singing together, the bond it produces as we raise our voices in unison—or parts—to praise the Lord. Many times, as a choir director, I've arrived at practice on Wednesday nights very tired and wondering what I could offer in terms of inspiration to those who faithfully gave of their time each week. But something happens inside of us when we praise God through music. Our spirits are refreshed as we turn our hearts and attention to God's praise, and I leave choir practice feeling uplifted and revived.

Even if you don't consider yourself "choir material," be sure you make your own "joyful noise" before the Lord. It is a paradox that when we are tired or discouraged, without energy, the act of praise, which requires energy, is that which renews us! That is the uniqueness of our relationship with God. Praising him is necessary for our well-being. He doesn't need our praise, but we need to praise him. Thanking him, praising him, helps us to keep our focus on him. And what a privilege it is to offer up praise to Almighty God, especially when we join with other believers in praise! God delights in our corporate praise on a much higher level than my household canine choir amuses me. So have your private praise in your quiet time and add your soprano "woo," your "alto howl," or your "joyful noise" in shared praise when you fellowship with other believers. God will bless you many times over for your offering of praise.

Dear God,

Thank you for the privilege of fellowshipping with other Christians through praising you in music. Let our sacrifice of praise be acceptable to you, O Lord, our Redeemer.

No Matter How Far We Get from Home, the Master's Voice Calls Us Back

> My sheep hear my voice, and I know them, and they follow me.
>
> John 10:27

My voice student walked into my front room studio and casually remarked that my dog was loose outside in the front yard. Oh, no! I went flying past my student only to see Lady, my beautiful Collie/German Shepherd Dog mix, heading down the street. Knowing I couldn't run as fast as the dog, I grabbed my car keys and sped out of the driveway down the street after her. She got about a quarter of a mile down the street and then turned into an open area beside the elementary school.

She was already probably a hundred yards away by the time I spotted her from the street. I stopped the car and yelled out, "Lady!" Again, "Lady!" This time she heard me, turned around, looked at me, and came running back to me. It was as if there was a connecting line between us as she made her way back. All it took to bring her back to safety was recognizing my voice, which gave her the path home to my open arms.

How many times do we go barreling down life's highway, unfocused and without direction? We think at first what seems to be freedom is exciting until we

LADY

wind up in a foreign place without direction home. It is then that God calls us by our name. Just stop for a minute and imagine God speaking your name. It's very compelling to consider God calling out to us by name, and he will keep calling until we hear his voice over the din of our distraction. It is then that we remember whose we are—God's loved child—and we come running back to the peace and safety of his arms.

Dear God,

Thank you for loving us so much that you keep calling us until we hear your voice. Thank you that nothing in this world can ever sever the connection of your love for your children.

Cast All Your Cares on God . . . and Leave Them There!

Casting all your care upon him; for he careth for you.

1 Peter 5:7

Trying to bathe two dogs by yourself is not easy. First, you have to secure each dog, so they can't run away from you if they happen to see you preparing the big wash tub and realize something unpleasant is about to take place. Usually I would leave one dog in the house, so he couldn't see what was happening outside until the first dog was already washed—make that clean and humiliated (in their eyes, of course).

Then you have to secure the clean dog outside, so he won't go diving straight into the dirt to roll around and make himself into a mudcake of a dog. If all goes well, and the dog is secure, he will patiently stand there and wait till the second dog gets his bath. Then I can hold each dog's leash while we relax on the patio and wait for them to dry. Okay, that's The Plan. Sometimes, things don't go according to The Plan.

One warm, sunny afternoon, I had decided it was bath time. Everything went according to The Plan until I got to the part of securing the first dog after his bath, so he could (patiently) wait for the second dog to be bathed. I bathed my Collie/German Shepherd Dog, Lady, first and neglected to decide ahead of time where I would secure her. So I have an unhappy, sopping wet dog on my hands and nowhere to tie her up. I spotted my barbeque grill and decided it was stationary enough to be a good "hitching post."

Before I could even get Benji out of the house, Lady realized that she was stronger than the grill and took off running—with the grill still tied to her. It wasn't a big grill—not the professional kind—just the kind that stands on four spindly legs with the orange lid on it.

So here is Lady, fur still wet and clinging to her, running the length of the yard with the grill appearing to chase her from about two feet behind her. She was terrified! No matter how fast she ran, the grill was still behind her. (Evidently I had securely fastened her to the grill. The folly was that the *grill* was not securely fastened to anything!)

Finally, I was able to catch her, disengage her from the grill, and calm her down. I have laughed to myself so many times since then at the remembrance of seeing her running with the grill bumping along behind her. (Oh, by the way, the grill never seemed to work properly after that!)

How many times have we brought our burdens, our cares, to God, and then taken them back? We try to trust God at his word when he tells us to cast all our cares upon him, because he cares for us. But we grow impatient for God's timeline, just like Lady grew impatient for me to untie her from the grill. We think that maybe God needs a little help from us to handle our cares, so we go on our way with our cares still attached to us, chasing us like the grill appeared to be chasing my poor, terrified dog! When we fail to leave our cares with him and wait for his answer, we commit ourselves to carrying an unnecessary burden, which becomes exhausting both mentally and spiritually.

Only the Master can disengage us from the heavy weight of our cares and give us peace again. But we have to allow him to do this, and he so very much wants to. It is then we will have his peace which passes all understanding (Philippians 4:7).

Dear God,

Forgive my lack of faith when I try to help you carry my burdens after I bring them to you. Help me learn to fully trust your love for me and to leave my cares with you.

"Redeemed, How I Love to Proclaim It!"

> Forasmuch as ye know that ye were not redeemed with corruptible things, as silver and gold, from your vain conversation received by tradition from your fathers; But with the precious blood of Christ, as of a lamb without blemish and without spot.
>
> 1 Peter 1:18–19

Each time I adopt a dog to come into its "forever home," I know that I am redeeming it from its current circumstances to live in a home full of love and joy (and being remarkably spoiled). A couple of my dogs were picked from their litters as pups, and their circumstances were not (yet) dire.

However, Benji and Pluto were adopted as an intervention measure before they were to be taken to the pound. Sasha was adopted directly from the animal shelter. She had had some really cute puppies, and they had all found homes; but adult dogs are harder to place. I found Sasha through the helpful services of Petfinder.com at a local animal shelter. I'll never forget the day I went to get her. I paid the adoption fee, and they gave her to me. She was so hungry that she ate four Arby's sandwiches on the way home!

There was no up-front financial cost to redeem Benji and Pluto from their situations, and the adoption fee for Sasha was minimal. But Jesus

the day of adoption

paid an extreme price to redeem us to become adopted sons of God. In our scripture, Peter reminds us that the ultimate cost of our redemption was not silver or gold. It was the precious blood of Christ. Under the Old Testament Law, the people of Israel found redemption with God through a blood sacrifice. When Jesus came to earth, he paid the perfect and final price for our souls by shedding his blood and dying on the cross. Surely I am not worthy of this sacrifice! But God loved us so much that even while we were sinners, Christ died for us (Romans 5:8). Is it any wonder that one of the first Bible verses we are taught is John 3:16? "For God so loved the world, that he gave his only begotten Son, that whosoever believeth in him should not perish, but have everlasting life."

Dear God,

Thank you for sending your Son as the ultimate price for my redemption. I can never be worthy of this sacrifice, but never let me cease offering praise and thanksgiving to you for your love.

The Master Never Stops Looking for the Lost One and Rejoices When the Lost is Found

And he spake this parable unto them, saying, What man of you, having an hundred sheep, if he lose one of them, doth not leave the ninety and nine in the wilderness, and go after that which is lost, until he find it? And when he hath found it, he layeth it on his shoulders, rejoicing. And when he cometh home, he calleth together his friends and neighbours, saying unto them, Rejoice with me; for I have found my sheep which was lost. I say unto you, that likewise joy shall be in heaven over one sinner that repenteth, more than over ninety and nine just persons, which need no repentance.

Luke 15:3–7

Friday, February 27, 2004, I received a phone call at work to let me know that all three dogs were out of the backyard. Pippin and Pluto were missing. Sasha was loose in the front yard. My friend secured Sasha and said she would send her two children to search for the missing dogs. I dropped everything and drove home. That thirty-five-mile drive had never seemed so long!

I spent the rest of the day driving around the neighborhood with the windows down, calling out Pippin's and Pluto's names, hoping for some glimpse of them. While I was glad Sasha was safe, it was very lonely going to bed that night, just her and me, knowing that my two "boys" were out somewhere on their own. I could only ask God for his protection and watchcare over them.

The next day, Reagan, one of my sweet nieces, drove an hour from her home to help me look for the missing dogs. She helped me create lost and found notices, which we posted in several neighborhood stores, and searched with me in an empty field near my house. She left late in the afternoon, and I was so exhausted I sat down in the front room at my computer to play some mindless computer games.

About an hour later, my peripheral vision detected movement in the front yard. I almost dismissed it, but then I looked out the front door, and there was Pippin on the sidewalk! I burst through the door, almost scaring him, and called him by name to come inside. About that same moment, from an opposite direction, there came Pluto! I ushered them inside and then outside to the backyard where we rejoiced in their return, barking and yelling and hugging and howling! Needless to say, my neighbors heard us and came over to offer their congratulations on the dogs' safe return.

I will never forget the profound joy of the return of Pippin and Pluto. So many things could have happened to them, yet God delivered them back to me, extremely tired but uninjured. My joy, however, over the return of two missing dogs pales so much in comparison to God's joy over a repentant sinner. Jesus seemed to really want to emphasize this to us as he told three different parables to illustrate the rejoicing in heaven over a penitent soul. That's truly something to think about. Even the angels join with God in rejoicing over a sinner saved. I fear that we may lose this heavenly perspective in the middle of a world that thrives on sensationalism.

I was at an entertainment center recently to celebrate a niece's birthday, and I walked away from the bowling alley/ birthday party rooms/video games/pin-ball machines/rock-climbing wall/billiards room mega-center with total sensory overload. When this is what we've become accustomed to for celebrating, it seems to take an extra minute to really grasp the concept of the joy explosion in heaven when one who is lost is now found. And yet, this is Almighty God, Creator of the universe, our Maker, who is celebrating! Praise be to God!

Dear Father,

Thank you for loving me enough to call me in from the cold of life without you. I am humbled that you celebrate over my salvation!

Without Envy, Rejoice with Your Friends Over Their Good Fortune

Now his elder son was in the field: and as he came and drew nigh to the house, he heard music and dancing. And he called one of the servants, and asked what these things meant. And he said unto him, "Thy brother is come; and thy father hath killed the fatted calf, because he hath received him safe and sound." And he was angry, and would not go in: therefore came his father out, and intreated him. And he answering said to his father, "Lo, these many years do I serve thee, neither transgressed I at any time thy commandment: and yet thou never gavest me a kid, that I might make merry with my friends: But as soon as this thy son was come, which hath devoured thy living with harlots, thou hast killed for him the fatted calf." And he said unto him, "Son, thou art ever with me, and all that I have is thine. It was meet that we should make merry, and be glad: for this thy brother was dead, and is alive again; and was lost, and is found."

Luke 15:25–32

Part two of the story of Pippin and Pluto missing and then miraculously finding their way home is Sasha's reaction when they returned. As I burst out the door to welcome Pippin and then Pluto back home, Sasha stood in the door and growled at them! It was if to say,

"Didn't I engineer our escape from the backyard so you would get lost, and I could have our master all to myself? Now, here you are, back, and ready to spoil my party!"

I couldn't help but think about the older son's reaction to his brother's return in the parable of the prodigal son related in Luke 15. Yes, his younger brother had acted extremely selfishly by taking his inheritance and squandering it. But their father's love overlooked that and was simply glad that he was back and safe. The father had to reassure the older son that he had enough love for both of them.

Have you played the role of one of the brothers in this parable? Were you the one who had to go off and explore other lands and other lifestyles? Or were you the one who stayed close to home, never strayed from the church, and pretty much did what was expected of you? God has love enough for everyone, regardless of the paths our lives have taken. If you were the steady one, did you experience a little envy along the way for the explorations of your friends or your siblings?

Believe me, those explorations do take a toll on a life, and you, my stalwart friend, are stronger than you can imagine for your unwavering faith. So, rejoice with those who have returned to the fold and humbly value your sincere and steady service to the Lord, knowing that *he* rejoices in your faithfulness and has love enough for all who come to the Kingdom.

Dear God,

Forgive me when I throw myself a "pity party" and fail to rejoice over a friend's good fortune. Help me to trust in you for all my needs, knowing that you are faithful to love and care for your children.

O Ye Stiff-Necked Generation!

> Now be ye not stiff-necked, as your fathers were, but yield yourselves unto the LORD, and enter into his sanctuary, which he hath sanctified forever: and serve the LORD your God, that the fierceness of his wrath may turn away from you.
>
> 2 Chronicles 30:8

I always understood the term *stiff-necked* to mean stubborn and willful. It was a cognitive understanding, but it became experiential understanding when I put a leash on Chuckie, my first Siberian Husky, for his first walk with me. He was not happy about being made to submit to my control.

Not only did his neck bow up in protest, but the hair on his back bristled, and his eyes glared at me with betrayal as if I were no longer his playmate. And indeed I was not! Fortunately, it didn't take but a few blocks till he learned it was much more pleasant to walk beside me than to choke himself through his obstinate objection. We even progressed to him actually learning to heel and had many long, joyous walks together.

Such a vivid demonstration of being stiff-necked gave me pause to reflect on how God must see us humans balking at his will for whatever vain

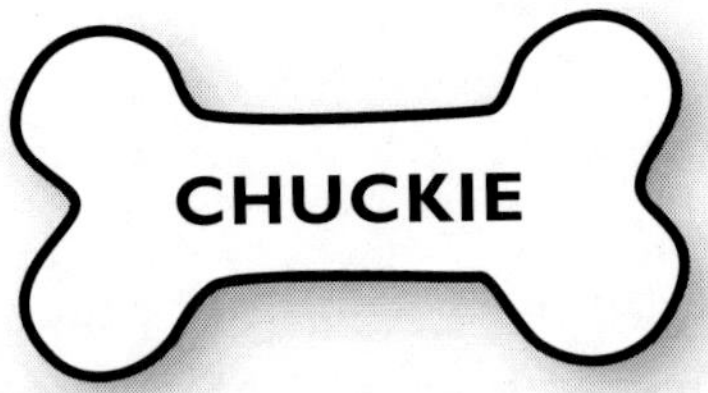

and my three nephews as children

and momentary path we would rather take than seeking his presence. I knew if Chuckie would yield to the leash what we could accomplish in terms of having special times together.

In our scripture, the Israelites were being urged to yield to the Lord and serve him, not only that God's wrath would be turned away, but also to experience his grace and compassion (v.9). When we are at peace with God and resting in his love, we have inner joy that gives us strength and sustains us through the adversities of life. I can think of no place that I'd rather be!

Dear Lord,

Forgive me when I willfully turn from you and seek my own way. Draw me back into the joy of walking with you as the center of my life.

No Pack Order in Heaven

> After this I beheld, and, lo, a great multitude, which no man could number, of all nations, and kindreds, and people, and tongues, stood before the throne, and before the Lamb, clothed with white robes, and palms in their hands; And cried with a loud voice, saying, Salvation to our God which sitteth upon the throne, and unto the Lamb.
>
> Revelation 7:9–10

The most obvious expression of canine pack order in my house has always been who eats first. I first noticed it when Benji, my usually meek Cocker Spaniel mix, could motivate Lady, a Collie/German Shepherd Dog twice his size, to yield her food bowl to him with just a low growl. Canine pack order can be determined by size, age, or seniority in the home (i.e., who got there first). Lady became Leader of the Pack when Benji died; after Lady died, Pippin became Leader of the Pack until Sasha, my second Siberian Husky, came to live with us.

Sasha was twice Pippin's size and quite a prima dona female. Nonetheless, Pippin didn't relinquish his Leader of the Pack status without protest. After several dog fights where Sasha pinned Pippin to the floor with apparent intent to go for the jugular, Pippin resigned himself to accord Sasha respect as new Leader of the Pack.

The Apostle Paul referred to himself as the chief of all sinners (1 Timothy 1:15). My only response to that is, with all my shortcomings and failures, "What does that make me?" And yet, I have hope, for I believe that in heaven we shall all have equal access to God on his throne. The Book of Revelations gives us a hint of what heaven will be like.

We will have the thrill of praising God with more people than can be counted. Earth's political and geographical divisions will be a thing of the past as we all stand before the throne of God wearing the white robe of the redeemed. This time, the crowd that waves the palm branches will not turn traitor by week's end but will spend eternity crying out with one heart and united voices that salvation comes from our God, who sits on his throne in majesty and power, and from the Lamb, our Prince, our Deliverer!

O Father Almighty,

How I long to join the throng and sing your praises forever! Give me purpose and determination to complete your mission for me during this earthly life so that I may enter heaven knowing I have run the course that you set before me.

Zealously Guard Your Relationship with the Master

Watch ye, stand fast in the faith, quit you like men, be strong.

1 Corinthians 16:13

Watch and pray, that ye enter not into temptation: the spirit indeed is willing, but the flesh is weak.

Matthew 26:41

At my house, I am always Leader of the Pack. This is necessary to maintain order and discipline. Beyond that, there is the canine pack order. At this present time, the canine Leader of the Pack is Sasha. The position of canine Leader of the Pack brings special privileges. Sasha eats first. If there is only one rawhide chewbone, it is hers. It doesn't matter that Pluto got to it first—all she has to do is walk up to him, and he will yield it to her with very little protest.

One particular privilege is that of having the closest spot in proximity to me. She sleeps closest to me. If she chooses, she alone has access to me for such time as she desires. She accomplishes this by placing herself in front of me and growling at either of the other dogs who may think about coming in my direction.

In her eyes, essentially, I am hers, and she shares me as she chooses.

This makes me think how zealously we should guard our relationship with the Master. So many temptations would cause us to let down our guard and interfere with our relationship with God. As Sasha stands "guard" over me and does not allow another one of the dogs to come close to me, we should also not allow anything to invade that which is holy. This can be done only if we are watchful of Satan's assaults. We must be vigilant and wary of his temptations. In our focal scripture, Paul exhorts us to be on our guard, standing firm in the faith. As we put on the armor of God, after we have done everything we can, again, Paul's appeal is to stand (Ephesians 6).

Dear God,

Help me to be wary of those little things every day that would cause me to jeopardize the priority of my relationship with you. When all is said and done, my choice is to stand firm in my faith.

My Dogs Protect Their Master, and I Can Count on the Master to Protect Me

> But let all those that put their trust in thee rejoice: let them ever shout for joy, because thou defendest them: let them also that love thy name be joyful in thee.
>
> Psalm 5:11

Besides companionship, my dogs provide an added dimension of security to my home. They are very territorial and extremely wary of potential "invaders." The ferocious-sounding barks and growls would certainly give any trespasser in his right mind pause to reconsider before attempting to enter my house.

On a more personal level, I have been touched by my dogs' efforts to protect me. We may be out for a walk, and if someone approaches a little closer than is comfortable, I have seen my dogs position themselves between the other person and me. For a while, my dear late mother lived with me before going to a nursing home. It is inevitable that two people living together will have a difference of opinion over something. It was at one of these moments that I felt something against my leg and realized that Lady had placed herself between my mother and me. She had sensed the discord and silently had moved in to protect me—from my feeble little mother!

What confidence we can have as we go through life knowing that God Almighty is our protector! Today's scripture tells us that we who have placed our trust in him can rejoice in knowing that he defends us and protects us. That doesn't mean that we are immune to trouble. It does mean that he ultimately is in control and has us in the palm of his hand. We can rest in the knowledge that "all things work together for good to them that love God, to them who are the called according to his purpose" (Romans 8:28).

Being diagnosed with breast cancer and going through the subsequent treatments of chemotherapy and radiation was an almost surreal time in my life. I hadn't felt sick when I discovered the cancerous lump. I had to keep telling myself over and over, "You have cancer." And still it was hard to believe—until the first chemo treatment had me sick and nauseous for three days.

But even during some of the worst times of treatment, when I didn't even have the strength to put out my garbage or walk to my mailbox, I had an assurance of God's hand on my life. While he didn't protect me from the earthly danger of getting cancer, I know that he certainly protected me during the treatments and that he is constantly caring for me and defending me. In this knowledge, I rejoice!

Dear God,

Thank you that we can have joy in knowing that you are our Shield and Defender!

LADY & BENJI

Can People Tell We Belong to the Master?

> Now when they saw the boldness of Peter and John, and perceived that they were unlearned and ignorant men, they marvelled; and they took knowledge of them, that they had been with Jesus.
>
> Acts 4:13

An older and wiser friend of mine was a houseguest for a night with me. Being a dog lover herself, she easily made friends with Benji and Lady. After petting them, she said this to me: "You can look into the eyes of your dogs and know that *they* know they are loved." What a concept! My love for my canine children is reflected in their eyes!

No one would argue that dogs don't show emotion. Wagging tails are a sign of happiness and well-being. Ears forward show signs of alertness. A yelp lets us know they are in pain. A gentle nudge from a soft muzzle when I've been preoccupied with TV or computer games reminds me they need playtime with me. I've often looked into the soulful eyes of my dogs and tried to convey my love for them by hugging them, patting their head, scratching behind their ears, or just talking to them softly. They respond by gazing at me with what I can only term as sheer devotion.

After healing the

lame man at the temple, Peter and John took the opportunity of the crowd to begin testifying about Jesus. This upset the Sadducees and the priests, and they locked up Peter and John overnight. The next day Peter and John were brought out to the rulers, elders, scribes, and priests, who asked them, "By what power, or by what name, have ye done this?" (Acts 4:7). (They were referring to the healing of the lame man.)

Peter and John answered them with true conviction regarding Jesus, proclaiming that there was no other name under heaven that could bring salvation (v. 12). They spoke so boldly and eloquently that the rulers and elders marveled, knowing that they were not learned men—just two rough fishermen. And today's focal scripture says that the rulers and elders and all those in the room acknowledged and recognized that Peter and John had been with Jesus.

When people hear us speak, can they tell we've been with Jesus? As we go throughout each day, doing the work that God has set before us, is it evident that we have spent time with Jesus? Just as my friend saw my love for my dogs reflected in their eyes, do people recognize Jesus' love reflected in our eyes? Can they see that we know we are loved by the Father God, the Creator of all living things? Does the testimony of our lives point the way to Jesus? Paul wrote to the Corinthians that we are the aroma, the fragrance, of Christ among those who are being saved and those who are perishing (2 Corinthians 2:15). Let us be the fragrance of life to all we know!

Dear God,

Let your love so shine in my life and in my eyes that others may see your truth and be drawn to you as our senses are drawn to a sweet fragrance.

More Than All Our Tithes and Offerings, God Desires Our Hearts

> And one of the scribes came, and having heard them reasoning together, and perceiving that he had answered them well, asked him, "Which is the first commandment of all?" And Jesus answered him, "The first of all the commandments is, 'Hear, O Israel; The Lord our God is one Lord: And thou shalt love the Lord thy God with all thy heart, and with all thy soul, and with all thy mind, and with all thy strength': this is the first commandment. And the second is like, namely this, 'Thou shalt love thy neighbor as thyself.' There is none other commandment greater than these." And the scribe said unto him, "Well, Master, thou hast said the truth: for there is one God; and there is none other but he: And to love him with all the heart, and with all the understanding, and with all the soul, and with all the strength, and to love his neighbor as himself, is more than all whole burnt offerings and sacrifices." And when Jesus saw that he answered discreetly, he said unto him, "Thou art not far from the kingdom of God." And no man after that durst ask him any question.
>
> Mark 12:28–34

I came home from choir practice one Wednesday night when Pippin was about a year old and opened the back door for him to come inside. The sight

Pippin

that greeted me was dreadful. There lay a dead rabbit—as close to the back porch as Pippin had been able to drag it. He was so proud! Tail wagging furiously, eyes bright with expectation, he had brought his master a great prize!

I cried out, "Pippin, what have you done? You've killed Peter Cottontail!" (I should mention that it was just a few weeks after Easter when this happened. Some poor child's Easter rabbit must have gotten loose and made the mistake of hopping into my backyard.) Gagging at the sight of the mangled rabbit, I got some plastic sacks and used them to scoop up Peter Cottontail, tied them securely, and rushed the ill-fated rabbit to the garbage can in the garage. I didn't scold Pippin—he was only doing what came naturally to him. I was truly sorry for the neighbor child who had lost the rabbit, but the fact that Pippin had brought the rabbit, his trophy, to me as a gift was rather endearing (after you got past the disgusting part).

Just as Pippin brought the rabbit as a love offering to me, so it is good for us to bring our tithes and offerings to God. He doesn't need them; it is for our benefit that we do this. God promised in Malachi 3:10 that if we would bring our tithes into his storehouse that he would open the windows of heaven and pour out more blessings than we could handle. I want that! I was raised with the concept of tithing—giving 10 percent of your income to God. I write my tithe check as I pay my bills after each payday. This has been a priority for me steadily for the last twenty years. I can testify that God has blessed me richly for this.

Once in a while, I forget to write my tithe check, and it is then that there is not enough money to pay the bills and doubly hard as a result of that to try and catch up on my tithe.

Somehow, though, when my tithe check is the first priority, there is enough money left to pay the bills that are due before the next paycheck comes. *But more than my tithe, God wants me.* He desires my heart, my mind, my soul, my strength. The scribe in our focal passage understood this as he commented that this means more to God than our "burnt offerings and sacrifices." Jesus commended the scribe's insight by telling him that he was not far from the Kingdom of God.

Dear God, I give you my all—my heart, my mind, my soul, my strength. I realize that it is only in giving you my all that I find true freedom, love, and peace of mind.

The Master's Scepter Is Always Extended to Us

> And it was so, when the king saw Esther the queen standing in the court, that she obtained favour in his sight: and the king held out to Esther the golden sceptre that was in his hand. So Esther drew near, and touched the top of the scepter.
>
> Esther 5:2

As any dog owner knows, dogs can speak volumes without ever making a sound, simply by looking at you through their soulful eyes. We see the intent look as they wait by the door to be let out. We see their eyes dance with excitement as we are about to offer their morning treat. We see the polite question in their eyes, "May I come up on the sofa and sit beside you?" Assuming I have the usual sheet or other protective covering over the sofa, the answer, of course, is always, "Yes." I find it interesting and endearing that they don't always take it for granted that they can come closer to me. Do they understand that it is a privilege to sit beside their master?

For Esther to come near the king, unbeckoned, was not just a privilege. It was a life and death matter! In an earlier chapter, Esther reminds her cousin Mordecai that it was against the law (and punishable by death) to enter the king's court without an invitation. But it was necessary for Esther to do this so that she could save the Jews from a plot to destroy every living person—man, woman, and child.

Esther herself was a Jew, although she had kept that secret while she was at the palace. Mordecai reminded her of her heritage and that possibly she was in her royal position by divine providence so that she could be instrumental in saving the Jews. So she put on her royal robes and risked her life to go and stand in the inner court opposite the king's throne. Our focal passage tells us that the king was pleased with Esther and held out his golden scepter to her to welcome her into his presence.

God's divine scepter is always extended to us! We are always welcome in his presence! Hebrews 4:16 encourages us to "come boldly unto the throne of grace, that we may obtain mercy, and find grace to help in time of need." What a privilege—that we may approach the throne of God, the maker of the universe, without fear and with the confidence and assurance of his love for us. Nevertheless, let us not take this license lightly but rather realize that it was a life and death matter—Jesus' sacrifice on the cross—that provided us this honor.

Dear God,

Thank you that you are always available to me. Let me never forget the precious blood of Jesus that paid the price for me to come directly to your throne.

I Am Fearfully and Wonderfully Made!

> I will praise thee; for I am fearfully and wonderfully made: marvellous are thy works; and that my soul knoweth right well.
>
> Psalm 139:14

God is quite an artist! Yes, I know, that's an understatement when you reflect on the grandeur of the Rocky Mountains, the overwhelming rush of the water at Niagara Falls, the raw, wild beauty of Alaska's glaciers, and the many rich colors of autumn's changing leaves in New England. This same God also created the Dachshund (the "wiener dog"), the spotted Dalmatian, and the corded Komondor. When you consider the wide varieties of dogs, you have to know God is an artist with a sense of humor!

I've sat and looked at my dogs so many times to marvel at his striking symmetry as he creates his creatures. Benji's, Lady's, and Pippin's tails were exactly as long as they were tall, stopping just short of dragging the floor. The facial markings on Pippin and Pluto form a mask with perfect arches that begin from the nose and go up over each eye. Lady was, and Sasha is, drop-dead gorgeous, with soft long hair and lovely coat patterns.

Yet on the other hand, God's sense of humor comes with a touch of whimsy, and I have to smile as I remember how Lady had one ear that was always pricked and one ear that was always hanging—a "flop ear," as I liked to call it. Lady had that famously long Collie nose, with a white streak going up almost to her eyes but not evenly. Pippin's tail is longer than either Pluto's or Sasha's, who both outweigh him by twenty-five and forty-five pounds respectively. I'm sure that God is lovingly amused as he touches his creations with uniqueness!

If he cares so much about dogs and other animals who can't commune with him, how much more must he care about *us?* We are made in his image, after his likeness (Genesis 1:26). I am humbled when I think that the Creator made me in his image. When you think about all the different human races and the uniqueness of every human face, it gives you reason to pause and ponder that we are all God's children; he made each one of us, and we are all made in his image.

Jesus said to his disciples, "Consider the lilies how they grow: they toil not, they spin not; and yet I say unto you, that Solomon in all his glory was not arrayed like one of these. If then God so clothe the grass, which is today in the field and tomorrow is cast into the oven; how much more will he clothe you, O ye of little faith?" (Luke 12:27–28). So here we are, made in God's image, with the promise that he cares for us infinitely more than the picturesque flowers in the field. I exclaim with the Psalmist, "I am fearfully and wonderfully made!"

Dear God,

Thank you for making me in your image. Let me always be conscious of your love and care for me.

Help Me! I'm Somewhere I Shouldn't Be!

> The Lord knoweth how to deliver the godly out of temptations, and to reserve the unjust unto the day of judgment to be punished.
>
> 2 Peter 2:9

The spare bedrooms in my house are generally off-limits to the dogs. They have the run of the rest of the house, which is plenty of space. Every now and then, curiosity gets the best of them and they feel a need to be where they shouldn't. Every dog I've ever had usually made their foray into forbidden territory on a secret basis and managed to give me this look of "Who, me?" if I found something disturbed in the room. Every dog except Pluto, that is.

Pluto has a particular bark for when he finds himself in a place of trouble. The bark has a sound of an alert to it, combined with a little bit of innocence and some measure of urgency. The best way I can translate it to English is, "Help me! I'm somewhere I shouldn't be!" All I have to do is call for him to come back to the family room where the rest of us are, and he comes bounding back, glad to be back where he belongs.

Sometimes we find ourselves in places we shouldn't be. It may be a physical place, like at a party where there are illegal drugs.

It may be a social place, where friends are sitting around gossiping. It may be an emotional place, where the attentions of a member of the opposite sex may cause us to momentarily forget our spouse. It could even be a financial place, where we spend or gamble more than we have in the bank.

Today's scripture promises that God knows how to deliver the godly from temptation. He does this by sending his Holy Spirit to speak to us, giving us that warning of danger ahead, begging us to stop and turn around before we sin, and calling us to come back to God's presence and his family. When we do, what a relief! We know that life is only fulfilling when we are in the middle of his will. This is the time we find true freedom and contentment, with no urge to go where we shouldn't.

Dear God,

Thank you for calling me back from the brink of sin. I trust in you and you alone for all that I need.

Our Language Should be That of the Master's

> Only let your conversation be as it becometh the gospel of Christ: that whether I come and see you, or else be absent, I may hear of your affairs, that ye stand fast in one spirit, with one mind striving together for the faith of the gospel.
>
> Philippians 1:27

My cousin remarked to me recently that she had never given thought to the fact that dogs can show emotions. Her daughter had recently rescued a Sheepdog mix, and it is their family's first experience with a dog as part of the family. My cousin told me how her daughter has described Molly's joy when she arrives home from work. She is learning what we dog lovers and dog owners have known for a long time—these are creatures capable of a fairly high level of communication.

My dogs communicate with various inflections to their barks. One bark signals, "Sound the alarm! Intruders are near!" Another bark conveys the need to go outside for nature's call. Another bark impatiently cries out for my attention when I've been at the computer too long. I have learned the difference in these and other barks. But the dogs have also learned *my* language. My three dogs, in addition to knowing each other's names, know almost thirty commands, ranging from the basics (sit, shake, and drink) to more advanced (go back to bed, let's go for a walk, and where's your bone?). And so the longer they live with me, the more of my language they know.

Likewise, the longer we live knowing Christ as our Lord and Savior, the more *his* language should become a natural part of what we communicate to others. The Apostles Paul, James, and Peter all knew the importance of our speech. Each wrote about the necessity of keeping our speech holy as a reflection of he who is holy (1 Timothy 4:12, James 3:13, 1 Peter 1:15). Our expressions and our way of speaking tend to take on that with which we are associated.

A number of years ago, I began watching a late night show that contained some really foul language. As I watched this weekly program and was exposed to such ugly words, I began to notice that I allowed some of the expressions to creep into my conversation. I was disappointed in myself that I was so susceptible to what was fed into my brain, and I stopped watching this show. So if we take on bad speech habits as we are exposed to filthy language, does it not stand to reason that if we fill our hearts and minds with the Word of God, that what comes out of our mouths should reflect Christ? Therefore, let us commit ourselves to be holy in our speech and in our deeds even as he commanded us to be holy (1 Peter 1:16).

Dear Father,

"Let the words of my mouth, and the meditation of my heart, be acceptable in thy sight, O Lord, my strength, and my redeemer" (Psalm 19:14).

Home Is Where the Master Is

> In my Father's house are many mansions: if it were not so, I would have told you. I go to prepare a place for you. And if I go and prepare a place for you, I will come again, and receive you unto myself; that where I am, there ye may be also.
>
> John 14:2–3

As surely as moving is rough on the human family, it is almost always just as traumatic for the canine family members. When the movers came to move me back to Dallas from Miami, Benji watched as they packed up the entire household with this question mark on his face that asked, "Am I going to get packed too?" My mom had flown to Miami to make the drive back with me, so Benji was relegated to the backseat of my car. Nevertheless, he was content as he was with us. More recently, I moved from a home of seventeen years to be nearer family. All three dogs, Pippin, Pluto, and Sasha, had never known but one home.

Acclimating them to my new home was one of my primary concerns and priorities. With Sasha being the Alpha dog and the principal engineer of several of the last escape attempts at the prior home, I knew it would be crucial for her to adapt to the new home. If she did, I was sure "the boys" would follow her example. So I boarded Pippin and Pluto and kept Sasha with me at all times during the move. She got to spend the first night in the new house with me all by herself. She was edgy, but, again, she was with me and we slept in the same familiar bed that she knew. The next day, we picked up Pippin and Pluto.

When we got to the new house, they had a field day with all the new smells. But, again, there were familiar smells of furniture, clothes, etc., and they settled down very quickly. I was rather amazed. It was then that I realized that home for the dogs is where their master is.

In like manner, home for us is where the Master is. Sometimes, I get homesick when I am weary of earth's trials. I know my dear mother and brother are already home, and I look forward to that reunion. More importantly, I look forward to Jesus' welcoming arms. What a wonderful promise he made to us that he would prepare a place for us and come back for us. Whether his return for us is through our earthly death or by way of a chariot in the clouds, he promised that he would come for us so that we could be with him forever—at home with the Master.

But we must be ready to go home! We must repent from our sins and believe that Jesus died for us to take away our sins (Romans 5:8). It is only in giving him our lives and acknowledging him as our Savior and Lord that we are made acceptable to enter heaven (Romans 10:9). Therefore, we need to spend our time with him, sharing our burdens and our joys and relying upon him to take care of us. Then, when we finally arrive at home with the Master, our welcome will be like the comfortable greeting of old friends.

Dear God,

How I long to worship in your arms. Help me to make the most of my time here on earth until you call me home.

Our Father's Eyes Are Always Upon Us

> "Can anyone hide in secret places so that I cannot see him?" declares the Lord. "Do not I fill heaven and earth?" declares the Lord.
>
> Jeremiah 23:24

A colleague where I work has a miniature Yorkshire Terrier named Cupcake. Cupcake is a real princess. She has everyday dresses, dress-up dresses adorned with satin and sparkles, casual T-shirts, and even a trench coat for rainy days! Cupcake is alone all day, so she is left to herself to find entertainment. She does have a window where she can look out on the passing world and bark "hello" when the mailman leaves the mail outside.

My colleague tells me that in the morning she leaves Cupcake's toys neatly stacked on a bench beside the bed. When she arrives home, she finds the toys strewed about everywhere in the apartment! She remarked once how great it would be to be a "fly on the wall" and watch what happens when Cupcake is home alone. Cupcake's favorite stuffed toy, Mr. Turtle, is always the farthest from the bed, as if she takes great delight in furiously shaking it back and forth before she slings it across the room with all the strength her little four-pound body can muster!

Whether it is comforting to us or not, God *can* see us all the time. He knows what we do

CUPCAKE

in secret just as surely as he knows our public actions. In truth, our secret deeds are very rarely ever secret, to our closest loved ones or even our casual acquaintances. If we think that no one sees the overindulgent amount of food we consume when we are alone, they do see it sooner or later in the weight we gain. When we gossip with a close friend about others, knowing our words are confidential, how can we remain softhearted, seeing others through Jesus' compassion? If we are secretly unfaithful to our mate, it will eventually crack the intimacy of marriage and do irreparable harm to us, our family, and even those who may be looking at us for marital inspiration.

I remember when I was younger being told that I should judge my actions by whether I would want Jesus to find me in that situation when he returns for us. It is a good principle by which to live. So as you go about your daily routine, live your life in his light and consider whether your actions are worthy to be a witness for Christ. "Let your light so shine before men, that they may see your good works, and glorify your Father which is in heaven" (Matthew 5:16).

Dear Father,

Thank you that your eyes are always upon me. I want to live as if there were always a floodlight on my actions, that they would be honorable unto you.

SCOOTER

Let Your Love Be Genuine

> Seeing ye have purified your souls in obeying the truth through the Spirit unto unfeigned love of the brethren, see that ye love one another with a pure heart fervently.
>
> 1 Peter 1:22

No one cares for unfounded behavior change without warning. We don't treasure it in the people we deal with, and we certainly don't care for it with our canine associates. This story is about Scooter, an adorable Shih Tzu who belongs to my friend's husband. I would say he belongs to both of them, but Scooter makes it very clear whom he considers his master. He is absolutely devoted to his master, Ronney, and really just tolerates everyone else.

Scooter has that classic, sweet Shih Tzu face, with big soulful eyes that at the same time portray a little sense of impudence. If Ronney is not around, Scooter will let you pet him and play with him, and you will think that this dog likes you. But let Ronney enter the room, and this seemingly friendly dog can turn around in an instant and snap at you. (I know this from personal experience!)

What is one of the things we most treasure about those people we hold dear in our life? Consistency. It is difficult to have a healthy relationship with someone who allows themselves the luxury of moodiness. We never know what to expect from day to day with these people, and it can be quite taxing and tiring to try to cope with or humor them. Peter encouraged his readers to have unfeigned love for each other. In other words, love without pretense and without pretending—genuine. How can we do this? Through souls that have been made pure through obedience to the Holy Spirit's direction in our lives.

Dear God,

Forgive me my hypocrisies in my dealings with certain individuals. Teach me to really love other people, not just to pretend to care for them. Let this love grow in my heart as it reaches out to touch others.

Your Sins Will Find You Out

> You have set our iniquities before you, our secret sins in the light of your presence.
>
> Psalm 90:8

A few days ago I came home from the grocery store with two beautiful, fresh bagels—one covered and baked with asiago cheese, the other baked with cheddar cheese and jalapenos. (Jalapenos are *very* hot peppers. If you live in Texas, jalapenos are appropriate on just about any food at any time—breakfast, lunch, or dinner. We even have jalapeno jelly!) I was so tired when I came in that I didn't put away all the groceries, even leaving a few bags of staples on the floor to be put away the next day. When I came home from work the following day, there was no evidence that I had ever bought bagels, except for the remnants of a paper bag on the floor.

You guessed it! One of the dogs, most likely Sasha, had a field day with the bagels! There was no trace of either bagel anywhere. I worried about her consumption of the jalapenos, and I watched Sasha all evening to see if she was having any reaction to the spicy pepper. It seems that they took a little longer to get through her system, and the next morning bright and early she offered them back up to me. As she was heaving, I held the trash can without much compassion and said, "Yes, you're sick. That's what you get for eating *my* bagels!"

The history of David's adultery with Bath-

Sasha

sheba is related in 2 Samuel 11. In a nutshell, David saw Bathsheba, lusted after her, committed adultery with her, and strategically caused her husband to be killed in battle. He thought he had taken care of all of his loose ends to cover up his sins until the prophet Nathan came to him (see 2 Samuel 12). What David learned was that he could not hide his actions from the Lord and that his actions did indeed have consequences. What he had done in secret, Nathan brought into the light. When David thought that he as the King could "fix" his sin through an elaborate plan of deception and murder, he learned that even kings answer to Almighty God.

To his credit, David showed true and sincere repentance for what he had done, but that didn't keep him from God's judgment. Nathan related God's word to David by reminding David of all God had given to him. If that wasn't enough, Nathan told David that *God would have given him even more.* Yet David allowed himself to be caught up in a web of sin, and for that, Nathan told him that not only would his child with Bathsheba die, but the sword would never leave David's household. And indeed, it never did. (See 2 Samuel 13–18)

If King David, whose heart was described as being perfect before God (1 Kings 11:4), had to face the consequences of his sins, who are we to think that we can escape the consequences of our own sins? At best, we can model our repentance after David's plea in Psalm 51 and cry out, "Have mercy upon me, O God!" We must acknowledge our sins and ask God to restore to us the joy of our salvation. Only then can we be an effective witness for him!

O merciful God,

Forgive my sins that create a chasm between you and me. Give me wisdom and strength to learn from the consequences of my sins.

Just as Our Dogs Give Us Unconditional Love, the Father Loves Us Just as We Are

> But God, who is rich in mercy, for his great love wherewith he loved us, even when we were dead in sins, hath quickened us together with Christ, (by grace ye are saved;) and hath raised us up together, and made us sit together in heavenly places in Christ Jesus.
>
> Ephesians 2:4–6

One spiritual truth I realized from my first Siberian Husky (and every dog after that) was his totally unconditional love for me. I got Chuckie at a time when a relationship was on the rocks. My self-image was pretty bruised, and I was not feeling good about myself at all. Chuckie was just a puppy when I got him, and he was full of joy and love and playfulness.

It was clear that his best moment of the day was when I arrived home from work, and he would greet me with kisses and excited barks. And perhaps this has always been one of *my* best moments of the day—coming home to a chaotic welcome of barks and wagging tails. My dogs have been perfect lessons of the wonder of unconditional love. They have never cared what I looked like—whether I gained weight or lost weight. They don't know the difference in a little dust on the floor or if the house is spic-and-span clean.

They have loved me just the way I am with no judgment whatsoever.

God's love for us is unconditional—so much so that he loved us while we were dead in our sins. What does it mean to be dead in our sins? There is no life apart from Christ. All our shortcomings and transgressions against God, our family, our friends, and our fellow man separate us from his life and his love. Yet, he did look on us in all our sin-filled ugliness and *loved us anyway!* He loved us enough to die on the cross for us. And God's same life-force that raised Jesus from the dead courses through us when we accept his gift of love and life. Amazing! Why would he do this? So that he could demonstrate his grace and love for us and allow us to sit in heavenly places with Christ Jesus. My cries of unworthiness are surpassed by shouts of praise and adoration for the One who offers us this wonderful gift of love and life!

Dear Heavenly Father,

Thank you for your all-encompassing love for me that looked beyond my natural sinfulness and loved me anyway. Thank you for the life-gift of your Son, Jesus Christ. May I never forget the cost of this gift and may I never boast in anything or anyone, save you.

Just as Canine Ways Are Not Human Ways, Human Ways Are Not Divine Ways

> For now we see through a glass, darkly; but then face to face: now I know in part; but then shall I know even as also I am known.
>
> 2 Corinthians 13:12

I sometimes wonder what my dogs are thinking as they watch me go about my days. It must seem strange to them that I have to keep changing my "body coverings" (also known as "clothes") rather than having one fur coat to wear all the time like they do. It must also seem strange to them that I don't eat like they do. Their manner is very direct—mouth to food. Not only do we use our "paws," we put something long and shiny in our paws to spear or scoop the food to our mouths. I'm sure the dogs think our method is very inefficient compared to theirs! But, of course, we humans consider ourselves much more advanced than the animals.

If we ever start thinking that we have God figured out, that is the time to step back for a dose of humility! Paul was writing about love and declared that while many things, including knowledge, will pass away, love never ends (v.8). He goes on to describe our earthly knowledge as imperfect (v.10) and compares it to looking into a dim mirror versus being face-to-face.

Have you ever looked into an old mirror that cast a blurry reflection? That's the level of comprehension we have regarding spiritual things.

During the course of writing this book, my computer system crashed. I had a couple of warnings by way of strange things happening on the computer screen, so I saved hard copies of what I had written so far. Was it a coincidence that the computer crashed within one hour of my completion of the chapter that provides the plan of salvation? As I related this to a dear cousin, we questioned whether God had kept the computer from crashing long enough for me to write that particular chapter, or had Satan become so incensed that I was reaching out to non-believers through my writing that he caused the computer to crash? And my cousin ventured the idea that there was spiritual warfare going on over my computer.

Indeed, how much spiritual warfare goes on all the time of which we are not aware or can comprehend? "For we wrestle not against flesh and blood, but against principalities, against powers, against the rulers of the darkness of this world, against spiritual wickedness in high places" (Ephesians 6:12). This brings us back to the promise in our focal passage—that we will have complete spiritual understanding when we at last are face-to-face with the Master.

Dear God,

Thank you for the promise of complete spiritual revelation when we finish our earthly journey and stand before your throne. In the meantime, shield us from Satan's fiery arrows as we seek to do your will and share your truth with others.

It Not Only Hurts Us, but the Master Also When We Refuse His Love

> And he fell to the earth, and heard a voice saying unto him, "Saul, Saul, why persecutest thou me?" And he said, "Who art thou, Lord?" And the Lord said, "I am Jesus whom thou persecutest: it is hard for thee to kick against the pricks." And he trembling and astonished said, "Lord, what wilt thou have me to do?" And the Lord said unto him, "Arise, and go into the city, and it shall be told thee what thou must do."
>
> Acts 9:4–6

Scooter is the sweetest-looking Shih Tzu you could imagine. But his temperament defies his looks, because he is only consistently loyal to his master and not anyone else, including his master's wife. When I visit Scooter and his human family, I want so badly to pet him and scoop him up in my arms and love him. But he will not have it!

I love to good-naturedly pick at him and tease him because I am stubbornly holding on to the belief that he may actually one day come to accept me and love me. So far, that belief seems to be folly, as it was only recently that, as I was messing with him, he leapt from his chair and went after my feet with full fury. Fortunately, I had on some especially thick shoes, or it would have meant some very mangled toes! Scooter's anger is incredibly misplaced at me. He is only hurting himself by not accepting my love and attention. If he would only let me hold him, I would give him hugs and kisses that no little doggie could refuse!

Saul (later Paul) was going after Christians in the Roman Empire much like Scooter went after my feet. He was on the warpath! Saul went to the High Priest and got permission to take out his fury on the disciples and believers in Damascus. As he was on the Damascus Road, God stopped him dead-on with a blinding light and asked him, "Saul, why are you persecuting me?" Saul was, in the very name of the Jewish faith, going after believers in God, as manifested in Jesus Christ!

But he didn't even recognize God in that encounter, so he asked, "Who are you, Lord?" And the Lord said, "I am Jesus, whom you are persecuting: it is hard for you to kick against the pricks." What does it mean to "kick against the pricks?" It's best translated in today's language as fighting against something only to be hurting your own self in the long run. Saul was not only hurting himself in his quest to hurt the new believers, but he was also hurting the Lord. God loved Saul, even in the face of his fervent persecution.

Can't you just imagine how anguished Jesus' voice must have sounded as he took such dramatic measures to get Saul's attentions? During his earthly ministry, Jesus grieved over Jerusalem, the city of God's chosen people, by crying out, "O Jerusalem, Jerusalem, thou that killest the prophets, and stonest them which are sent unto thee, how often would I have gathered thy children together, even as a hen gathereth her chickens under her wings, and ye would not!" (Matthew

23:37). Can you hear Jesus crying out to you—wanting to gather you to himself and love you, even in your rebellion? What can our response be to such compassion? We can learn from Saul's reaction by saying, "Lord, what would you have me do?" and obey accordingly.

Dear Father,

Please remind me that I, like Saul, am hurting both you and me when I find myself in misguided rebellion against your Word. I do love you, and I always want that to be the centering truth of my life.

It Grieves the Master When His Children Quarrel Among Themselves

> What causes fights and quarrels among you? Don't they come from your desires that battle within you?
>
> James 4:1

It can happen in an instant—two peaceful, sweet dogs turn into snarling predators going for each other's jugular vein—usually over something so simple as life's basics: food, water, or a chew-bone. Nothing scares me more than to see two creatures who are like children to me attacking each other. I'm happy to say that it happens very rarely, but it is nerve-shattering when it does.

A few times there has been bloodshed, and I wonder how they keep from killing each other because their fury is so intense. I've heard that the best thing to do to break up a dog fight is to pour water on them—I just use whatever's in my hand at the moment. The last time it happened to be a can of ravioli, so there were little raviolis and red meat sauce all over the dogs and my beige carpet! There's always an eerie quiet after a fight. I scold the one who started the fight and show preference to the one who was attacked to further impress upon the instigator my displeasure with him or her. I can tell that withdrawing my favor hurts the dog's feelings, so I don't prolong the punishment. They are usually very quick to get beyond the momentary disagreement—much more so than most humans!

It grieves me so that my sweet pups could attack each other. And if it breaks my heart over a dogfight, how much more must our heavenly Father be grieved when his own children, bought by his Son's blood, quarrel among themselves? Church dissensions are not restricted to any one denomination. Unfortunately, I've seen selfish actions and reactions in several denominations and churches where I have served. In one church, albeit a seeming cliché, the fight literally ensued over where the organ would be placed in the sanctuary! In another church, the argument was over where the piano would be placed. Christians, fervent in their faith, dependable in their deeds for Christ, can get caught up in the most frivolous issues, and the result is a crippled church! We as believers are sealed by the Holy Spirit (Ephesians 4:30). To be sealed is to be airtight, waterproof, so that that which is sealed cannot be damaged. Satan would love to damage the Church and us individually as Christians. He cannot have us because we are sealed by the Holy Spirit. However, he can certainly damage our effectiveness, and one of the easiest ways for him to do this is to damage the fellowship among Christians, which results in a marred and ineffective witness to a lost and searching world. Oh! If we could only be more aware of his onslaughts and rebuke him in the holy and wonderful name of Jesus!

Holy God, forgive us when our own desires become more important than a spirit of unity with our fellow Christians. Help us to be on guard against the Evil One, as he seeks to damage your church and your children.

Rest in the Arms of the Master

> Trust in the LORD, and do good; so shalt thou dwell in the land, and verily thou shalt be fed. Delight thyself also in the LORD: and he shall give thee the desires of thine heart. Commit thy way unto the LORD; trust also in him; and he shall bring it to pass. And he shall bring forth thy righteousness as the light, and thy judgment as the noonday. Rest in the LORD, and wait patiently for him: fret not thyself because of him who prospereth in his way, because of the man who bringeth wicked devices to pass.
>
> Psalm 37:3–7

I'm sure that the phenomenon of a child falling asleep in a parent's arms is well-known to many. Most children have total faith in and dependency on their parents for their safety and comfort. Dogs also rely on their masters for their safety and comfort. In my experience, one thing unique about dogs, though, is that they really never completely relax when you're holding them. It seems that there's always one ear perked for your slightest move, and that they are not completely at rest.

One night, however, Pippin was allowing me to hold and cuddle him. Now Pippin, as anyone who has ever known him agrees, has "issues." He really only loves me as his sole human, and even then he will turn on me if I happen to place my hand on him unexpectedly. So the fact that he was even cuddled in my arms was special, and I was being very still.

Then he let out a long sigh, and his body weight relaxed into total sleep. How precious that was to me! This sweet creature, who I sometimes have longed for him to be more of a "lap dog," trusted me so much that he let himself fall asleep in my arms. It was a humbling feeling, a feeling that I didn't want to ever move from that spot and disturb him. How God longs for us to rest in him! He promises time after time that we can trust him and find rest in him. God surely knows the value of rest. "And on the seventh day God ended his work which he had made; and he rested on the seventh day from all his work which he had made. And God blessed the seventh day, and sanctified it: because that in it he had rested from all his work which God created and made" (Genesis 2:2). Back in the "good ol' days," no one worked on Sunday. Almost all of the stores were closed, and there was no work done around the house. After a week of hard work, Sunday was for church and resting. In today's world, that's hard to imagine, isn't it?

In the Old Testament, there are numerous references to finding rest. Among them are:

- 1 Kings 8:56a: "Blessed be the Lord, that hath given rest unto his people Israel, according to all that he promised."
- Ruth 1:9: "The Lord grant you that ye may find rest."
- Psalm 116:7: "Return unto thy rest, O my soul; for the Lord hath dealt bountifully with thee."
- Jeremiah 6:16a: "Thus saith the Lord, Stand ye in the ways, and see, and ask for the old paths, where is the good way, and walk therein, and ye shall find rest for your souls."

God even wants the land and our animals to rest! "And six years thou shalt sow thy land, and shalt gather in the fruits thereof: But the seventh year thou shalt let it rest and lie still; that the poor of thy people may eat: and what they leave the beasts of the field shall eat. In like manner thou shalt deal with thy vineyard, and with thy oliveyard. Six days thou shalt do thy work, and on the seventh day thou shalt rest: that thine ox and thine ass may rest, and the son of thy handmaid, and the stranger, may be refreshed" (Exodus 23:10–12).

Jesus said, "Take my yoke upon you, and learn of me; for I am meek and lowly in heart: and ye shall find rest unto your souls" (Matthew 11:29). God *wants* us to rest, and he delights in providing it to us—not just physical rest, but rest for our souls. He *wants* us to trust him. It makes sense, doesn't it? Why should we not put our trust in God Almighty, Maker of heaven and earth? Then why is it so hard for us to do it?

When I was a teenager, I painted a poster for a walk that our youth group made. The poster said, "Let go and let God." It hung in my bedroom for years. Sometimes I think I still need that poster in my room, reminding me that I need to let go of all that's holding me back from trusting God to provide the rest that is so valuable to our well-being. You, too, can find rest. Just take the advice of my poster and "Let go and let God."

Dear Heavenly Father,

How my spirit longs to be centered in the rest of your arms. Thank you that you love us so much that you want to provide rest unto our souls.

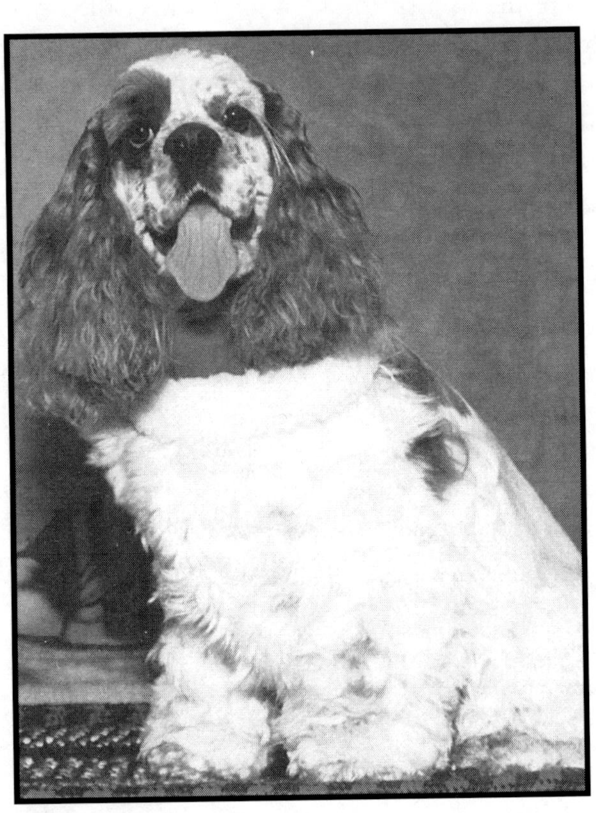

FRECKLES

All Dogs Don't Go to Heaven

> After Job had prayed for his friends, the Lord made him prosperous again and gave him twice as much as he had before. The Lord blessed the latter part of Job's life more than the first. He had fourteen thousand sheep, six thousand camels, a thousand yoke of oxen and a thousand donkeys. And he also had seven sons and three daughters.
>
> Job 42:10, 12–13

The death of a loved pet can be devastating. A dear friend of mine lost Freckles, a Cocker Spaniel. Freckles was a faithful and loving part of her family for over thirteen years. He had that famously sweet nature known to Spaniels and would make himself cozy between her and her husband when it was bedtime. My friend has a soft, kind heart, and she truly grieved at the loss of her canine friend. Those of us who have lost our puppy dogs recognized the sadness in my friend's heart and grieved with her.

Twenty years ago, when I lost my first Siberian Husky in a horrible accident, I searched the Scriptures for solace and comfort. Chuckie was my first dog as an adult, and the first dog that died that I truly grieved for. I wanted so badly to believe that I would see Chuckie again, that he was waiting for me in heaven.

As I read through the book of Job, I noted

the loss of his herds of oxen, donkeys, sheep, and camels. Then came the terrible news of the loss of his children. But Job was faithful in his trust of God and never spoke against God, regardless of how bad things got. In the end, God blessed Job with more herds than he had before. God also gave him more children. God didn't bring his former herds or his children back to life, but he did bless Job with new herds and more children.

While the idea of a "dog heaven" is comforting to us, I have found no Scripture references to support the idea that we might see our pets again in heaven. As much as I believe that dogs are communicative creatures with feelings and emotions, I also believe that they are finite beings without a soul. They enrich our lives for a certain number of years, and then they are gone. It is very natural to grieve for the loss of our pets. We had a relationship with them, and they endeared themselves to us. But don't close your heart to allowing another of God's creatures to come into your life. If Job's heart had remained closed and bitter after the loss of his children and his wealth, God would never have been able to bless "the latter part of Job's life more than the first." Give God your heartache, and, while he won't bring our beloved pets back to us, he will bring new pets into our lives to give us joy and love.

Dear God,

Thank you for bringing such special puppy dogs into my life for whatever time that you have deemed right. I am blessed for the love and companionship that each dog has brought me.

I Believe; Help My Unbelief

> Now faith is the substance of things hoped for, the evidence of things not seen.
>
> Hebrews 11:1

I've always been fascinated by guide dogs and the relationship between the blind handler and the dog. I can't imagine what it's like not to have your sight, much less to have to rely on a dog to guide you safely through city streets and crowds of people. The amount of trust that a blind person must have for his guide dog is beyond my comprehension. I know that both the dog and the handler have been through training, individually and with each other.

Nevertheless, I would think it literally requires steps of faith for the visually challenged among us to work with their guide dog. We have a blind gentleman at our office who has a Golden Retriever guide dog. We have all been taught "dog etiquette" so that we know not to try to pet or play with the dog when he's with his handler, because the dog must remain in "working" mode. It's very difficult to do this, because what's better in the middle of a stressful day at the office than to be able to pet a soft, blond, furry coat of smiling canine?

The writer of Hebrews brings us the classic definition of faith in chapter 11. Faith constitutes believing in what has not yet come to pass, believing in what has not been seen. I believe, based on my faith in Jesus Christ and the fact that I have asked him into my life as my Lord and Savior, that I will go to heaven. Heaven is not a physical place on earth that I can visit. Yet I believe it exists. Other than the reflection of his shining presence in someone's eyes, I have never seen God. Yet I believe he exists. I accept the concept of the Trinity—that the Father, Son, and Holy Spirit are the Triune God. Yet my limited earthly imagination cannot understand that completely.

To believe when you cannot see, understand, or touch is faith. The disciples asked Jesus to teach them to increase their faith, and he responded by telling them that if they had just as much faith as the size of a mustard seed (approximately 1 mm in diameter), they could move mountains! (Luke 17:5–6). Indeed, from the tiny mustard seed comes a very large tree. This says to me that we all have the potential to have a lot of faith. It is already inside the believer. We simply have to let it grow and blossom in our hearts.

Dear Father,

I believe. Help thou my unbelief (Mark 9:24).

God's Timing Is Always Right

> To every thing there is a season, and a time to every purpose under the heaven: A time to be born, and a time to die; a time to plant, and a time to pluck up that which is planted.
>
> Ecclesiastes 3:1–2

Three weeks after losing my first Husky, my ladies' Bible study teacher called to tell me of a little dog that was on his way to the pound if another home couldn't be found for him. I was still grieving for the loss of my companion, Chuckie, and couldn't even imagine opening my heart to another dog. She persisted, though, and even said she would go get the dog and bring him to me.

Although she had not known me but a few months, she evidently knew me better than I knew myself. The scruffy, meek little "Cocker-mutt" that I named Benji was just what my poor, lonesome heart needed. I often considered how the timing of his need for a new home coincided with my need for a new companion. I asked myself (and God), "Did Chuckie have to die so Benji could have a home?" I knew that was not really the case. But God has always made a way for another dog to come into my home after the loss of one.

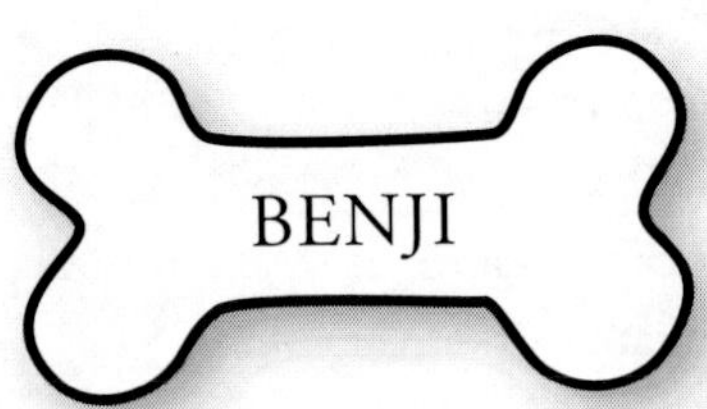
BENJI

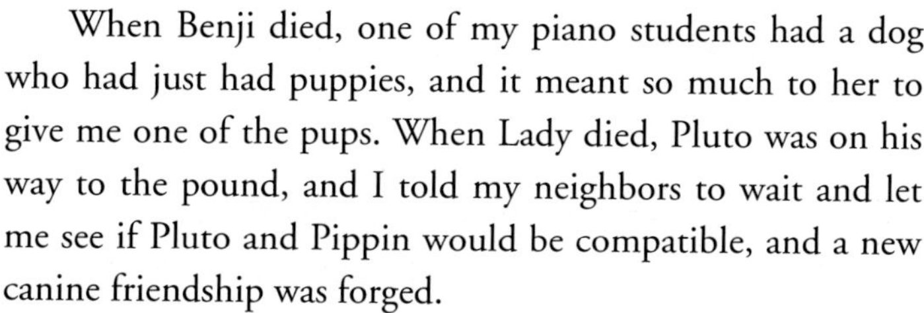

When Benji died, one of my piano students had a dog who had just had puppies, and it meant so much to her to give me one of the pups. When Lady died, Pluto was on his way to the pound, and I told my neighbors to wait and let me see if Pluto and Pippin would be compatible, and a new canine friendship was forged.

If only we could trust God in our own lives for his perfect timing! We offer up our prayers with a timetable that we have designed and ask God to please accommodate our needs as we see them. Sometimes God moves us in a direction that we don't understand at the moment, but is revealed to us down the road. Such was the case for me when I left one church as music director to go to another church in the same capacity. It was almost two years later that I had a revelation about one of the reasons God had prepared this particular place of service for me.

I remembered then the sermon I had heard years ago comparing our lives to a parade. While we are ground level and can only see each float (life event) as it passes by, God can see the whole parade—our whole life. His view of the big picture can give us confidence that we are in his hands, and we can lay hold of the promise of Romans 8:28: "And we know that all things work together for good to them that love God, to them who are the called according to his purpose."

Heavenly Father,

I'm so thankful that we can trust in you for your perfect timing in our lives. Help me to remember this when I get impatient for your will to be done on earth as it is heaven.

The Master Will Never Give Up on Us or Forsake Us

> When thou art in tribulation, and all these things are come upon thee, even in the latter days, if thou turn to the Lord thy God, and shalt be obedient unto his voice; (For the Lord thy God is a merciful God;) he will not forsake thee, neither destroy thee, nor forget the covenant of thy fathers which he sware unto them.
>
> Deuteronomy 4:30–31

The first time I ever left Pippin alone in the house, he was eight months old and it was only for ten minutes. When I returned (and I stress that I was only gone ten minutes), I found one of my sofa cushions completely destroyed and apparently half-eaten! Pippin was so proud of himself, wagging his tail even as I scolded him. Cost for rebuilding the cushion and recovering the sofa: $145. (Oh, did I mention that this was ten days before I was to host our family's Christmas gathering?) A number of my acquaintances remarked that perhaps I should be getting rid of Pippin, but I've never been one to give up on a dog.

Shortly after Sasha came to live with us, I was trying to find a way to confine her, as she had that typical Husky "escape artist" trait. I tried the guest bathroom, and she only lasted a few days in there before she literally clawed the door open and tried to "dig" her way out into the rest of the house by tearing up the carpet by the bedroom door all the way down to the cement foundation. This same day, she apparently also tried to get outside, because the blinds at either window were destroyed, as if she was attempting to claw through the window. She was a one-dog demolition squad!

Again, suggestions were made to me that perhaps Sasha should be returned to the animal shelter from whence she came. But I believe in the "forever home" premise when you adopt a dog, and I determined to persevere with her. I began crating her, and eventually her maturing as well as settling into the household finally enabled me to leave her in the house loose without fearing that I would come home to find the whole house in shambles.

I am so glad that God doesn't give up on us. Time after time in the Scriptures, he makes the promise that he will not leave us or forsake us. He promised Joshua that he would be with him even as he was with Moses (Joshua 1:5). On his deathbed, David promised Solomon that he could count on God to be with him until he had "finished all the work for the service of the house of the Lord" (1 Chronicles 28:20). The writer of Hebrews encourages us by reminding us that God has said he would never leave us or forsake us (Hebrews 13:2).

One thing that I am most encouraged by as I read through the Scriptures is how *human* God's servant's are. Abraham, David, Peter—all with their own individual flaws, and yet we most associate them with the great things they did for God. God was patient with these patriarchs of the faith and never gave up on them. And so he is with us—he will never give up on or forsake us. Hallelujah!

Dear God,

Thank you that even when others would write us off as a lost cause, you are patiently, constantly, and consistently there for us.

The Master Is Available to Us 24/7

> And, lo, I am with you always, even unto the end of the world.
>
> Matthew 28:20b

I find great contentment in being a homebody, with my dogs stretched out on the floor around me. I would love to be a stay-at-home mom to them, but, like most everyone else, I have to work so that I can provide a home for the critters and me. I've always found it interesting that the dogs seem to know the difference between weekends and workdays. Even if our routine has been disrupted for a number of days, the dogs seem to easily adjust back to my work schedule and go to their respective places of repose as I am about to walk out the door.

My friend Cate's dog, Cupcake, is a little more persistent, though, when Cate is getting ready for work. She wants more playtime! So, one by one, she brings her toys to the door where Cate is getting ready. She stands at the door, drops the toy, and gazes up at my friend. She saves Mr. Turtle for last, as if to say, "Okay, I'm offering up my *favorite* toy. Won't you please take time to play with me?"

While we cannot be available to our sweet pups all the time, God is always with us and available to us. He *always* has time for us. We can take great comfort from today's

Scripture that he is with us even to the end of the world. In Psalm 139, the psalmist declares that he cannot be anywhere but that the Lord God is there with him (Psalm 139:5–10). God is not limited by earthly constraints but is omnipresent—a concept that I accept by faith without need for scientific explanation.

Jesus promised that he would "pray the Father, and he shall give you another Comforter, that he may abide with you for ever" (John 14:16). The Scriptures are full of promises that God is with us and will be with us. We are never alone! So be encouraged as you go about your day and know that God is right there alongside you, strengthening you and supporting you in your daily activities.

Heavenly Father,

Thank you for the reassurance that you are always with us and always available to us. Let me not take your presence lightly or in vain but live as you are truly standing there beside me.

Restore the Joy of My Salvation

> Restore unto me the joy of thy salvation; and uphold me with thy free spirit.
>
> Psalm 51:12

Recently my usually loving dog Pluto aggressively went against Pippin, his senior in the pack order both by age and precedence in the home. Pluto is much larger than Pippin, and, as usual, the subject of the dispute was something as basic as food. It is not Pluto's place to go against pack order, and after rescuing Pippin, I scolded Pluto severely, and he knew he had messed up badly.

In fact, the dogs and I went to bed that evening with Pluto still in disfavor. I went off to work the next day with Pluto knowing he was still in trouble. By the time I came home, I decided enough time had passed from his misdoing that it would be pointless to continue to punish him by withdrawing my affection. So I greeted him with the same love to which he was normally accustomed. For the next several days, he had a sweet meekness about him as he approached me, and he seemed to revel in the restoration of my demonstrated love for him.

I heard a saying once that went like this: "If you feel far from God, guess who moved." We can take comfort in knowing that God does not withdraw his love from us when we have sinned. If we feel separated from God, it is not God's fault. It is our sin that stands between Him and us. We must ask forgiveness from God for our wrongdoings before we can experience the joy of his presence and salvation. But unlike the way I treated Pluto by withholding my affection, God does not hold back. In fact, he takes the lead by extending his love and forgiveness before we even ask it!

The Bible tells us of so many times when God takes the first step toward restoring our relationship with him. It begins as early as God looking for Adam and Eve in the garden of Eden after they had eaten of the Tree of the Knowledge of Good and Evil. The pattern continues when God searched out Cain to ask of Abel's whereabouts and confronted Cain with killing Abel.

Even then, when Cain whined to God that his life would be in peril without God's favor, God had compassion and placed a mark on Cain so that anyone would see that Cain had God's protection. God's taking the first step in restoration culminated in his offering up of his only Son to be the path of deliverance for our sin. How do we respond to this divine demonstration of love? We can take our cue from those who have gone before us and simply cry out, "Have mercy upon me, O God!"

Dear Heavenly Father,

Thank you that even in our unworthiness you reach out to us to bring us back into the joy of your salvation.

The Master Wants Us to be Kind to One Another

> Which now of these three, thinkest thou, was neighbour unto him that fell among the thieves? And he said, "He that shewed mercy on him." Then said Jesus unto him, "Go, and do thou likewise."
>
> Luke 10:36–37

I have a dear friend who has the most tender heart of anyone I know. To visit Carol's home is like visiting a petting zoo. Carol has an affinity for animals of all kinds. She has dogs, cats, cows, miniature donkeys, ducks, a goose, and even a pet bird named Larry. From the smallest to the largest, she loves them all, and they all seem to know it. Some of her brood she has chosen; some of them she has taken in as strays, only to become loved members of her household.

Carol found Wiley in the middle of the highway starved, dehydrated, and abandoned. The best she can determine is that he is a senior dog that someone just threw away to die. You have to wonder how many others passed by Wiley while he was lost and homeless but ignored him, didn't have time for him, or didn't want to chance getting themselves dirty. Now Wiley is happy and content within Carol's household, and

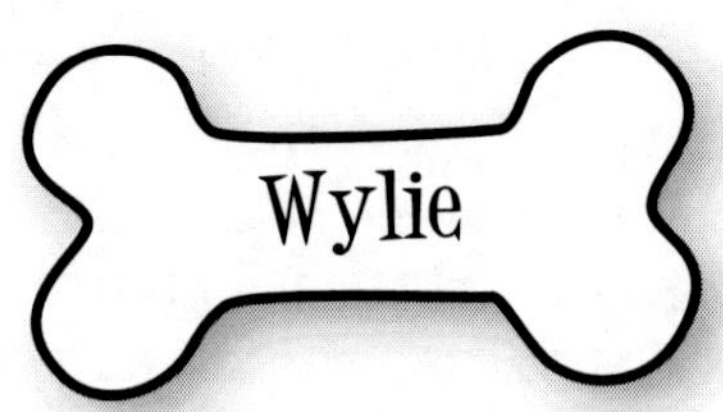

Wylie

he knows he is loved. Carol says that Wiley is the gentlest dog she has ever known.

It is important for us to take care of the animals that share God's earth with us. But even more important is the need for us to look after our fellow man. Second to the command to love God with all our heart, soul, strength, and mind is the command to love our neighbor as ourselves. What precipitated Jesus' parable of the Good Samaritan in the preceding verses to today's focal passage was a discussion of who do we actually call our "neighbor." It is most comfortable to think of our "neighbor" as a mirror image of ourselves. They look like we do, they dress like we do, and, for the most part, they act like we do.

But in Jesus' parable, the "neighbor" was a Samaritan! For centuries, the Samaritans were despised by the Jews, to the extent that a journey would be made longer in order to bypass Samaria rather than go through it. That's how much the Jews reviled the Samaritans! So for the Samaritan to be the hero, the "neighbor," in Jesus' parable was extremely controversial in Jesus' time. It can be controversial for us to look beyond our circle of friends and acquaintances to consider someone unkempt or uneducated as our neighbor. But after looking away, take time to look back and remember that this too is a soul for which Jesus' gave his precious life and see the lost and forgotten through God's eyes of love.

Dear Father,

Forgive me when I turn and look away from someone whom you love as much as you love me. Remind me that even as I've received mercy from you, I must show your mercy to others.

Are You Wearing Your Spiritual Collar?

> Take my yoke upon you and learn from me, for I am gentle and humble in heart, and you will find rest for your souls. For my yoke is easy and my burden is light.
>
> Matthew 11:29–30

One message a dog's collar conveys to the rest of the world is that the dog has a master. If we see a dog loose on the street with no collar, we view that dog as a stray. Conversely, if we see a dog loose on the street wearing a collar, we assume that dog escaped from its owner and is in need of being returned home. Collars—at least for my dogs—are necessary even within the home. They are the means by which I can guide my dogs, and a manner in which I can maintain order and discipline. Many times I use their collars to be able to pull the dogs close to me so that I can pet them and show them affection. Even though collars can sometimes be construed as a constraining device, they are actually a sign that someone has cared enough for the dog to place a mark of ownership on it.

In today's focal passage, Jesus encouraged the crowd to take his yoke upon them. The imagery of a yoke on oxen was very familiar to the people of Jesus' time. It was used to join the oxen together and usually consisted of a heavy wooden crosspiece with two bow-shaped pieces, each of which enclosed the head of one of the oxen. The yoke was a means of controlling the animals as they performed work for the people. Contrary to the image of a device used for a beast of burden, Jesus assures us that his yoke is easy and his burden is light. He promises that his yoke—his collar, if you will—in its spiritual reference, will bring peace to our souls. There is a difference in dogs and us, though, when it comes to wearing the yoke.

Whereas a human places a collar on a dog whether the dog wants it or not, Jesus *invites* us to take his yoke upon us. We do this by acknowledging him as our Savior and Lord and seeking his direction for our lives. And, as he promised, it is then that we find peace and serenity in his gentle leadership.

Dear Father,

Every day help me to remember to take your yoke upon me, so that my actions will reflect that I am yours.

SHELBY

Only the Master Can Bring Peace to the Wild, Restless Soul

> Then they went out to see what was done; and came to Jesus, and found the man, out of whom the devils were departed, sitting at the feet of Jesus, clothed, and in his right mind: and they were afraid.
>
> Luke 8:35

Shelby was a stray that wandered onto the property of a fence company with a rope around her neck, obviously abused from the last human with whom she'd had contact. Her natural reaction was to strike out in angry self-defense if a human came near. Deciding that the dog was just too wild and aggressive to try to save, the owners of the fence company decided she just needed to be killed to put her out of her misery.

They were trying to decide whether to shoot her or run over her when Staci intervened. Staci is the daughter of my dear friend Carol, whose house is an unofficial refuge for lost and stray animals. Staci began to leave food by her parked car at the fence company for Shelby. Cautiously, Shelby approached to eat the food. After a few days of finding food beside the parked car, Shelby began to wait in Staci's parking space for Staci to arrive at work.

Once Staci won Shelby over, she took her to her mom's house and left her there for Carol to care for when she came home. At first, the dog shied away from Carol and would not come near her. Carol knelt near the animal and continued to talk to it in that soft, kind voice of hers. Slowly the dog took a step forward—then another, and another as Carol tried to reassure her.

At last Shelby let Carol pet her, and she kept on petting her as she spoke to her. Once she lifted her hand just for an instant, and Shelby drew back, as if expecting Carol to hit her. Again, she had to win her back with her calm and gentle ways. As Shelby has gratefully settled into Carol's household, Carol reports that Shelby has shown none of the aggression that jeopardized her life at the fence company.

Until we know Jesus as our Lord and Savior, there is a wild stray in all of us. It may manifest it in "riotous living," or it may just be a void feeling in our hearts, knowing that *somewhere* there is peace to be found for our weary souls. Today's verse is the end of the account of a man possessed by many demons. He was homeless and naked and lived outside the city in the tombs. When he saw Jesus, he cried out, "What have I to do with thee, Jesus, thou Son of God most high? I beseech thee, torment me not" (v. 28).

Jesus recognized the peril of this man controlled by his demons. He cast the demons out of the man, sending them into a nearby herd of pigs. The demons caused the pigs to rush off the cliff of the mountain into a lake, where they were drowned. Those who witnessed this spectacle went back into town and told what had happened. And as today's verse attests, when the townspeople came out to see for themselves, they saw the former wild man "sitting at the feet of Jesus, clothed, and in his right mind."

Is your soul restless? Are you searching for peace in your world? Sometimes our first instinct of self-defense is to back away in anxiety and mistrust from anyone who would attempt to bring us relief. So were the reactions of Shelby, who backed away from Carol's tender hand; and the demon-possessed man, who cried out to Jesus not to torment him. But God reaches out to us with patient and gentle love. You can be assured that you can have peace in your heart, mind, and spirit, even though the world about you may seem out of control. Jesus can lift the despair from your soul as surely as he sent the demons into the pigs. Give him the chance to give you his peace that passes all understanding (Philippians 4:7).

Dear God,

Thank you for calling us in from the wild to give our restless souls your peace.

MOLLY

God Is Faithful to Us, Even When We Are Not Faithful to Him

> Here is a trustworthy saying: If we died with him, we will also live with him; if we endure, we will also reign with him. If we disown him, he will also disown us; if we are faithless, he will remain faithful, for he cannot disown himself.
>
> 2 Timothy 2:11–13

This is the story of Molly and Otis. Molly, a Sheepdog mix, was adopted from a shelter by my cousin's daughter, Lauren. Molly has won the hearts of all of Lauren's family, as she is very sociable. Molly's neighbor is Otis, a Terrier mix. Otis is an outside dog and really enjoys the times that Molly is outside. He will come and sit next to the fence to greet her. Then they will run up and down the length of the fence several times, barking "hello" and "how-do-you-do." Molly soon tires of this and ambles off to explore other parts of the yard, leaving poor Otis at the fence, patiently waiting for her to return for some more fun.

Does this behavior sound familiar? God is always available to us. When we find the time, we enjoy fellowship with him and bask in his love and care for us. We are truly thankful for his blessings and the gift of his Son, Jesus. However, long before God is done taking pleasure in our company, we get sidetracked by life and its accompanying responsibilities. We leave God patiently waiting for our return to "the fence," so to speak, as we wander off to explore other interests. But just like today's scripture says, God is always there, waiting for us, for even "if we are faithless, he will remain faithful."

Dear God,

Thank you that you are faithful even when I am not. Draw me to "the fence" daily and often for life-giving fellowship with you.

Our Spirits Inherently Long for the Master

> For we know that the whole creation groaneth and travaileth in pain together until now. And not only they, but ourselves also, which have the first fruits of the Spirit, even we ourselves groan within ourselves, waiting for the adoption, to wit, the redemption of our body. For we are saved by hope: but hope that is seen is not hope: for what a man seeth, why doth he yet hope for? But if we hope for that we see not, then do we with patience wait for it.
>
> Romans 8:22–25

My good friend Marianna and I recently went on a vacation together. Leaving town requires each of us to make plans for the care of our dogs. Almost anyone who has a canine companion can tell you that their dogs know when their master is about to go away. They recognize suitcases—the packing of the suitcases and the loading of the suitcases into the car. By the time the luggage is taken to the car, any dog I've ever had is beside himself with excitement, knowing that, eventually, he will also be loaded into the car too!

After taking my dogs to the place where they were to be boarded, I arrived at Marianna's house. Normally, her little Toy Poodle, BeBe, enjoys me playing with her, but not so on this particular morning! BeBe

BeBe

was fraught with excitement and expectation. She knew her master was about to leave and that she also was going on a trip. By the time we got in the car, all eight pounds of her was quivering with anticipation, and she was emitting moans and groans, whines and whimpers, the likes of which I've never heard! These continued until we arrived at the kennel where she would be boarded.

BeBe's sounds and behavior called to mind today's scripture. Just as BeBe was groaning in expectation, so also do we as Christians "groan within ourselves, waiting for the adoption, to wit, the redemption of our body." There is a vacuum inside us that can only be filled by the presence of Jesus Christ. Although we are distracted by "the sin which doth so easily beset us" (Hebrews 12:1), we naturally long for companionship with God. And while the Holy Spirit indwells us on this earth, filling us with God's presence, our "adoption" as God's children will only be fulfilled completely when we see him face-to-face.

Dear Father,

I look forward to that time when you say, "Well done, my child, welcome home." Until then, comfort my inward groanings with the knowledge of your presence and the hope of my eternal adoption.

We Honor the Master When We Minister in His Name

> Then shall the righteous answer him, saying, "Lord, when saw we thee an hungred, and fed thee? or thirsty, and gave thee drink? When saw we thee a stranger, and took thee in? Or naked, and clothed thee? Or when saw we thee sick, or in prison, and came unto thee?" And the King shall answer and say unto them, "Verily I say unto you, Inasmuch as ye have done it unto one of the least of these my brethren, ye have done it unto me."
>
> Matthew 25:37–40

At fifty pounds, Lady, my Collie/German Shepherd Dog mix, was relatively large but very gentle. During the time my mother lived with me prior to going to the nursing home, Lady gave her good companionship. Because of Lady's size and her instinctive protectiveness, I never worried about my mom alone in my house with the doors unlocked while she waited for Meals on Wheels and other visitors and friends.

After Mother went to the nursing home, I took Lady to see her a few times. The other nursing home residents delighted in Lady's visits as well. They all enjoyed petting her and watching her do her best trick, which was to shake hands. Pet therapy has been utilized for over thirty years to minister to nursing home residents. A dog's companionship can have such therapeutic effects as lowering blood pressure, increasing physical activity through the act of stroking the back of the dog, and relieving stress, as well as generally improving a person's self-esteem.

Certainly if dogs can effectively minister to hurting individuals, we as God's hands here on earth can do the same. We live in a world that cries out for compassion and a tender touch. The same human conditions that Jesus talked about two thousand years ago still exist today. The hungry are not just pictures on the television in a faraway land; they are in the heart of America. There are people who have spiritual thirst and don't even recognize it as their need of Jesus. The homeless can be seen wandering about any time of the day or night. Prisons overflow with individuals who made very bad choices. We build more clinics and hospitals every day to treat our growing number of people who suffer from real physical ailments brought on by the stress of our culture.

Jesus told his listeners that any time they ministered to the suffering souls around them, they had actually ministered to him. What an honor! To *minister* to the King of kings! As we reach out to the hurting among us, let us always remember Jesus' words, "Inasmuch as ye have done it unto one of the least of these my brethren, ye have done it unto me."

Dear God,

Give me a heart of compassion for the afflicted around me. Help me to see your face in those to whom I seek to minister.

It Is Only Through the Master's Love That We Can Love and be Loved

There is no fear in love; but perfect love casteth out fear.

1 John 4:18a

Dogs and children have an innate understanding of their entitlement to be loved. You see it in a child as he snuggles into his mother's embrace. My dogs express this by luxuriating in the time that I pet them and show them affection. As I pet them from head to tail, they begin to stretch and then roll on their back, so I can rub their tummies. (Have you ever seen a dog that didn't like to have his tummy rubbed?) They will stay in that position for as long as I have time to spend with them. If I start to move away, they will turn and stretch closer to me, as if begging me for more.

Somewhere between the innocence of childhood and the caution of adulthood, we lose that wondrous sense of the entitlement to be loved. The simplicity of our belief that we are lovable is chiseled away by experiences that break our hearts. It can happen through the rejection of other children on the playground; it can happen through a parent leaving because of divorce; it can happen through the loss of a first love; it can happen through the betrayal of an adult who uses our trust to exploit us. We lose the resiliency of our capacity to love so that by the time we reach adulthood, we have walls that act as fortresses to our hearts.

God gave us the desire to both give and receive love. Only he can heal us from the inside out by our acceptance of his overwhelming love for us. As we open our hearts to him more and more, the walls around our hearts begin to crumble, and we see the world through his eyes of love.

O God, how I long for the joy of a heart that is open to love. Let me trust you daily for the confidence that, through you, I am loved and I can love.

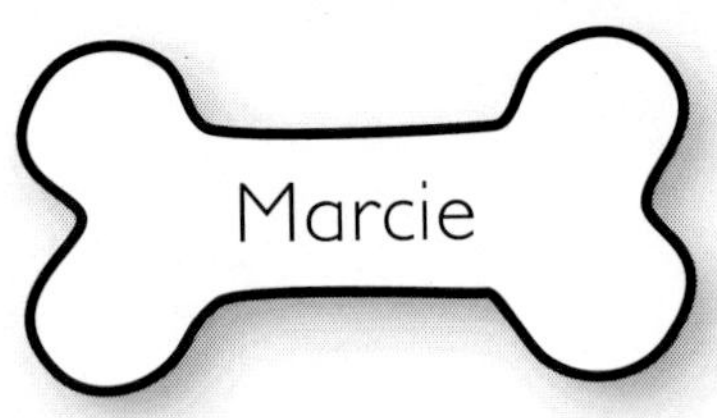
Marcie

The Master Makes Us Beautiful Within, Which Makes Us Beautiful on the Outside

> Your beauty should not come from outward adornment, such as braided hair and the wearing of gold jewelry and fine clothes. Instead, it should be that of your inner self, the unfading beauty of a gentle and quiet spirit, which is of great worth in God's sight.
>
> 1 Peter 3:3–4

My neighbors recently adopted a boxer named Marcie. Marcie, at eighty-five pounds, the size of a small person, has the characteristic broad, chiseled face of the boxer breed. She is a good watchdog. The mere sight of her standing on her hind legs with her massive jaws, barking at visitors who arrive at the front door, immediately commands healthy respect for this dog.

There is nothing elegant about Marcie—she doesn't have a long, flowing coat of hair; her tail is docked so that it's just a little wagging stub; and she has the typical Boxer underbite that gives this breed its unique, expressive face. Once Marcie understands that you are her friend, she becomes a real sweetheart and, with her deep brown eyes gazing at you as you pet her, she actually becomes a beautiful dog.

This is what Peter is trying to tell us—that our beauty should come from within. Like Marcie, we may look a little rough on the outside. Our spirit, though, tempered by the love of Christ, is reflected on our countenance, and we actually become more attractive. For who *isn't* attracted to love, grace, and compassion? More valuable than any beauty make-over is the make-over Christ wants to perform on our hearts. Give him a chance to take your heart and transform it. You will have a new concept of what beauty truly is!

Dear God,

I'm ready for my make-over. Let your love and grace be beautifully reflected on my face and in my life.

The Master Wants Us to Help Each Other Bear Our Burdens

> Rejoice with them that do rejoice, and weep with them that weep.
>
> Romans 12:15

I lost my only brother to a sudden, massive heart attack. No event in my life from that time to the present has ever rocked my world in such a devastating manner. My mother and father divorced when I was a child, so my big brother was not only my brother but a father-figure and a friend as well. If we could be any closer, we had become so after our mother's death, just twenty months prior to my brother's heart attack.

When I arrived home from the hospital where he died, many friends were there to offer me support. Pippin, my little American mutt, has *always* had issues with other humans in the house. A meek sweetheart in my one-human, three-dog family, he could not deal with any other humans in the house and always barked nonstop in genuine frustration. But this one particular day, when I arrived home with my heart breaking and friends were trying to comfort me, Pippin sat silently by my side. As people milled about and frequently came over to hug me, Pippin maintained his silent vigil by my side. There was no question that Pippin was deeply aware I was very sad, and he did the only thing he knew to do—sit beside me in heartfelt loyalty.

We could well heed what even a dog knows—the value of standing beside a friend or loved one in total, heartfelt loyalty and sympathy when their world is disintegrating about them. In Paul's letter to the Romans, he follows his rich dissertation about the hopelessness of our sinful nature and the incomprehensible wonder of God's saving love for us with practical instructions for the believers. Couched among these pragmatic one-liners is the brief encouragement: "Rejoice with them that do rejoice, and weep with them that weep." Paul understood how important it is that we stand by each other and help each other keep standing. Consider this the next time your friend needs comforting—that simply being there and maintaining vigil in heartfelt loyalty and compassion becomes God's loving arms made tangible here on earth.

Dear Heavenly Father,

As much as you have sent friends to stand with me in rough times, please let me be deeply aware of hearts in need around me.

The Master Encourages Us to Join Together in Intercessory Prayer

> Verily I say unto you, Whatsoever ye shall bind on earth shall be bound in heaven: and whatsoever ye shall loose on earth shall be loosed in heaven. Again I say unto you, that if two of you shall agree on earth as touching any thing that they shall ask, it shall be done for them of my Father which is in heaven. For where two or three are gathered together in my name, there am I in the midst of them.
>
> Matthew 18:18–20

My niece told me about their family dog when she was a child. Tasha, an American Eskimo Dog, was snow white and very beautiful. One day Tasha accidentally fell into their swimming pool and could not get out. She cried and clawed and could not get the family's attention to rescue her. Sensing a fellow creature's peril, one by one the dogs in the neighborhood joined in the distress call. It was not until all the dogs together made such an alarming clamor that my niece's family realized something was wrong and pulled Tasha to safety.

There is power in consensus and agreement. Whether it's neighborhood dogs all together sounding an alarm, a political rally endorsing a candidate, or Christian believers joined together in prayer, we can see the power of unity. Jesus knew the power of prayer and wanted us to

TASHA

know the power of praying in one accord. He promised us that if (only) two or three were in agreement on anything that they should pray to God, and it would be done. I have seen this happen so many times in my own life. A number of years ago, I lived in Miami, Florida, far from my Dallas-area home. Miami had not been kind, and I wanted to move back to Texas very badly. The job market was tight, and I needed to secure a job that would pay my moving expenses. In August, a friend, my mother, and I made a covenant to pray every day that God would make a way for me to come home. I suggested that we ask God to make it happen by Christmas. My friend countered with Thanksgiving (exhibiting much more faith than I had). Answered prayer: I was home by November 8th—even before Thanksgiving! *Praise be to God!*

Many Christians can testify to God's answers to community prayer. These testimonies build us up together in faith and remind us of God's grace and mercy. He is actively involved in our lives and wants *us* to be actively involved with him. Think of this the next time you have a need and gather a couple of believers around you for prayer and supplication to the Lord.

Dear Father, let me not forget nor ever take for granted how you want to show us your goodness and love for us through the granting of the request of two or three who are in agreement in your name.

We Should Be Ready for When the Master Returns for Us

> For the Son of Man is as a man taking a far journey, who left his house, and gave authority to his servants, and to every man his work, and commanded the porter to watch. Watch ye therefore: for ye know not when the master of the house cometh, at even, or at midnight, or at the cock-crowing, or in the morning: Lest coming suddenly he find you sleeping.
>
> Mark 13:34–36

Scooter's master had been out of town all week, and Scooter had spent the week visiting his brother, Rylie. It was a fun household, and the teenager Connor had given him some real special attention, but Scooter missed his master. When the master's wife came to get him and take him home, Scooter just knew he would see his master at any moment. He sat staring at the front door, waiting; but his master didn't come.

It wasn't until the next day that his master, Ronney, arrived, and Scooter barked for joy as he welcomed his master home.

Jesus compared his second return to that of a man leaving his house for a long journey and empowering his servants to keep the household running smoothly. This was done by each servant taking care of his own responsibilities. And so has Jesus left us empowered to keep his world together until he returns, with each one of us carrying out the work that he has gifted us to do.

Jesus cautioned us not to be found sleeping when he returns. Surely this is meant in a broader concept (and not literally sleeping), as in not doing the work that he would have each of us do. Consider what it is that he would have you do. Is it to build up and equip the saints? Is it to speak his truth to the unsaved? Is it to teach children about our loving Savior? Ask God today to show you his work for you until Jesus returns for us.

Dear Heavenly Father,

Thank you that you have vested in us the responsibility for doing your holy work. Let us not be found sleeping when you return. Even so, come, Lord Jesus (Rev. 22:20b).

The Master Rejoices in the Brotherly Love of His Children

> Be devoted to one another in brotherly love. Honor one another above yourselves.
>
> Romans 12:10

When I boarded Lady and Pippin at my vet's, the staff sometimes had interesting stories for me when I returned. One example was Pippin's protectiveness of Lady. Pippin adored Lady, and even though she was the Alpha dog and bigger than him, he would try to protect her. The vet's staff told me that he would get very upset when they would come to take Lady for her bath, but he would settle down once they returned her to the run that they shared.

Lady eventually died, after providing me with fourteen years of wonderful companionship. When I began to remove her lifeless body from the den where I had sat with her while she struggled with her last breaths, Pippin began to bark hysterically. It was rather touching that he didn't want me to take away his friend, even though I'm sure he sensed that she was dead.

Proverbs tells us that "there is a friend that sticketh closer than a brother" (Proverbs 18:24). I have been blessed with a number of close friendships. They have been there for me at so many of life's junctures. However, I think have never felt such an outpouring of love and care as during the period of time that I was battling breast cancer through surgeries, chemotherapy, and radiation. When I had my first two surgeries, several of my co-workers took personal time off from the office to come and sit at the hospital with my family while I was in surgery.

I never had to drive myself the forty-two miles from my home to the hospital for sixteen chemo treatments, because friends were there for me. As I lay in bed incredibly sick and nauseous from the chemo, my girlfriends came to my house and answered my phone, cleaned my refrigerator, and did laundry. When I was too weak to even walk to my mailbox, my neighbors brought me my mail and took out my trash.

When I was too sick to join my girlhood friends for a luncheon, they planned a trip in my honor for later in the year when I would be stronger and through with the most intense portion of my treatment. Seven of that special group of women made the celebration trip to Savannah, and I'm sure they have no idea how it helped me get through the months of treatment to be able to look forward to that trip.

Jesus told his disciples, "Greater love hath no man than this, that a man lay down his life for his friends" (John 15:13). Jesus showed us the ultimate love that a man can have for his friends. He gave up his life so that *we* could have life and have it abundantly. What a sacrifice! What an outpouring of love! As much as I know I have been blessed with earthly friends, I know also that, unworthy as I am, I have been blessed with life's greatest gift: Jesus Christ.

Dear Heavenly Father,

Thank you for how you show your love to me through my friends and family. Thank you for the greatest love, that of your Son, Jesus.

Only the Master Can Still the Storms of Your Life

> And when they had sent away the multitude, they took him even as he was in the ship. And there were also with him other little ships. And there arose a great storm of wind, and the waves beat into the ship, so that it was now full. And he was in the hinder part of the ship, asleep on a pillow: and they awake him, and say unto him, "Master, carest thou not that we perish?" And he arose, and rebuked the wind, and said unto the sea, "Peace, be still." And the wind ceased, and there was a great calm. And he said unto them, "Why are ye so fearful? How is it that ye have no faith?" And they feared exceedingly, and said one to another, "What manner of man is this, that even the wind and the sea obey him?"
>
> Mark 4:36–41

My female dogs have always been terrified of storms, especially at night. Since I know we are sheltered and safe from the storm, I try to keep on sleeping. But the dogs don't understand that. To get my attention, Lady would pace back and forth on the bed and then literally stand over my head. Sasha reaches out to me with her big paws and claws at my head—that's enough to wake you if you're sleeping! There is nothing I can do to stop the storm, but at least I'm awake and can cuddle the frightened dog.

Their actions are the canine form of the disciples' frightened reactions to the storm at sea. All they knew to do was to wake the Master. Granted, the boat *was* full of water. So it must have been a huge storm to alarm these seasoned fishermen. Nevertheless, they knew it was beyond their power to control, so they reached out to the one who could. And when he calmed the storm, the disciples asked themselves, "What manner of man is this, that even the wind and the sea obey him?" That "manner of man" is Jesus, Son of Almighty God the Father, who not only controls the storms at sea but the storms on land and the storms of your life, if you will let him.

How many believers can testify that Jesus carried them through the storms of their lives—and that no other power could have done that? My dogs look to me to still the storm, but I am human and have no power over the wind and the rain. But Jesus has all power! Jesus can see you through the storms that sooner or later come into every life. Cling to him, and he will see you through. He will not let you go. "For I am persuaded, that neither death, nor life, nor angels, nor principalities, nor powers, nor things present, nor things to come, Nor height, nor depth, nor any other creature, shall be able to separate us from the love of God, which is in Christ Jesus our Lord" (Romans 8:38–39).

Dear Heavenly Father,

What a comfort to know that you are in control of whatever storms come through our lives. When they do come, let me immediately reach out to you to hear you say, "Peace, be still."

Seek the Master with Your Whole Heart

> With my whole heart I seek you; let me not wander from your commandments!
>
> Psalm 119:10

My nephew's Jack Russell Terrier, Getty, is a sweet, comical dog. He's a little on the hyper side—not exactly what you would want if you were looking for a laid-back lap dog. Getty loves to watch television, and with my nephew's sixty-inch Mylar-screen TV, sometimes the characters almost seem Getty's size.

One day Getty was watching the series on the *Animal Planet* about the meerkats. He became so engrossed in the cute little animals that he *literally jumped through the TV screen* to become a part of the meerkat family! (Fortunately, Getty was not injured from his impulsive act since it was a soft-screen TV.) Note: Please do not encourage this of your dogs—or your children! Cost to replace the TV: $1800.00.

Oh! To be so overcome by the love of God that we would throw ourselves into our relationship with him just like Getty threw himself into the TV! Would that we might seek Christ with our "whole heart" as did the psalmist. What kind of impact could we as Christians make upon the world if we had that kind of passion for the Lord? Paul spoke to the

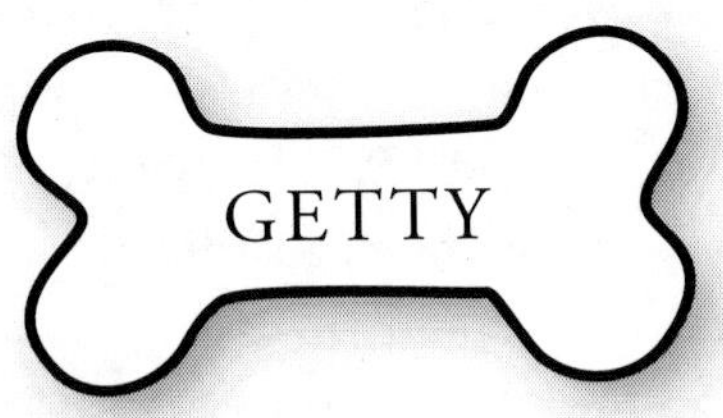
GETTY

Philippians about his single-minded purpose to know Christ in his letter to them: "For to me, to live is Christ, and to die is gain" (Phil 1:21). "Yet indeed I also count all things loss for the excellence of the knowledge of Christ Jesus my Lord, for whom I have suffered the loss of all things, and count them as rubbish, that I may gain Christ" (Phil. 3:8). Paul was sold out to Jesus. May he and the psalmist inspire us to be likewise in our walk with the Lord.

Dear God,

You know my heart. With my whole heart I seek you. Give me a thirst for you, O God, even as the deer pants for water (Psalm 42:1*).*

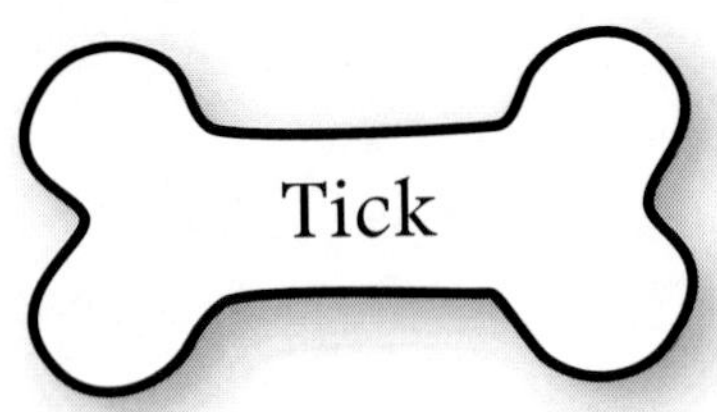
Tick

The Days of Our Lives Are in the Master's Hand

> Honor your father and your mother, that your days may be long upon the land which the LORD your God is giving you.
>
> Exodus 20:12

> He (David) died at a good old age, full of days, riches, and honor, and his son Solomon became king in his place.
>
> 1 Chronicles 29:28

> For David, after serving his own generation in God's plan, fell asleep, was buried with his fathers, and decayed.
>
> Acts 13:36

Tick belonged to Mark, the brother of my dear friend Scott. Tick got his name from all the ticks he was infested with when, as a stray, he wandered up to the family home with his Beagle mother. His official name was "Tickie Mutt," but most of the time he just answered to "Tick." Scott tells me that "the tiny mutt walked into our lives, and nothing was ever the same. He needed love and attention, and he gave it in return." The Dachsund/Beagle-mix became so much a part of his human family that he actually learned to speak one word of English—"Momma"—and even learned to open his own doors for himself—sliding or otherwise! After eighteen years, their beloved dog died, and Mark buried him in their backyard.

The average life span for a dog is between ten and fifteen years, so you can see how special Tick must have been to his family to live with them so long. God's Word seems to make specific statements about living long upon this earth. In the Ten Commandments found in Exodus 20, we are specifically commanded to honor our fathers and our mothers, that our "days may be long upon the land which the Lord your God is giving you." Although we are not told specifically King David's age at his death, the writer comments in 1 Chronicles that David died "at a good old age, full of days ..." Paul declares in the Antioch synagogue that "David, after serving his own generation in God's plan, fell asleep ..." There is a definite connection between honor, serving others through God's plan, and old age.

Does this mean that those who die young are not honorable or are not walking with God?" Absolutely not! My own brother, who died at age fifty-five, was one of the most honorable, Christian men I have ever known. There are many other men and women of God that we know were God's instruments who did not live long lives. But for those who do, what a blessing, what a legacy to our family, what a testimony of a life lived unto God, and what an encouragement to those still living—to witness a life filled with honor, a life yielded to God's plan, a life identified by others as God's servant!

O Father,

For however many years you may grant me, let it be said of me, as was said of David, that I served my generation according to your plan. Amen.

listen|imagine|view|experience

AUDIO BOOK DOWNLOAD INCLUDED WITH THIS BOOK!

In your hands you hold a complete digital entertainment package. Besides purchasing the paper version of this book, this book includes a free download of the audio version of this book. Simply use the code listed below when visiting our website. Once downloaded to your computer, you can listen to the book through your computer's speakers, burn it to an audio CD or save the file to your portable music device (such as Apple's popular iPod) and listen on the go!

How to get your free audio book digital download:

1. Visit www.tatepublishing.com and click on the e|LIVE logo on the home page.
2. Enter the following coupon code:
   014b-1f4e-a6da-4b96-3a66-664b-d936-f0c4
3. Download the audio book from your e|LIVE digital locker and begin enjoying your new digital entertainment package today!